St. Combs

My Buchan

St. Combs
My Buchan

by

David S. C. Buchan

The Pentland Press Limited
Edinburgh · Cambridge · Durham

The author wishes to express his sincere
gratitude to John S. Smith for the Foreword

© D. S. C. Buchan 1993

First published in 1993 by
The Pentland Press Ltd.
1 Hutton Close
South Church
Bishop Auckland
Durham

ISBN 1 85821 096 8

Typeset by Elite Typesetting Techniques, Southampton.
Printed and bound by Antony Rowe Ltd., Chippenham.

Contents

List of Illustrations

Foreword

David Buchan has assembled a literary *pot pourri* of good crack on St. Combs as he remembers it in his childhood and adolescence. From his insider knowledge, he unlocks the mysteries (for outsiders) of, *inter al.*, tee-names, fishing superstitions, temperance walks, village sayings and much more. It is clear from his school memories that, despite the isolation of seaboard village life, there was never a dull moment. The young folks indulged themselves in games and simple entertainment, a few of which might today be construed as low key vandalism without any evil intent. Right at the core of St. Combs was his familey's Post Office, locally described as the 'Harrods of the North' where phone messages and telegraphs were received and redistributed by various networks to the recipients. David writes engagingly of a time when fishwives travelled by train with their creels and when *potted heid* almost achieved the status of a delicacy. The book is rich in memories of individuals, local sayings and stories, all conveyed in an effective unpretentious style, and liberally enhanced by his own poems, written in the Doric. The text describes the hard times as well as the good, the latter perhaps epitomised by the rivalry between the three neighbouring villages over which could muster the most fur coats on the temperance walks. The hard times are best illustrated in the vagaries of fishing off a hostile shore with few boat landing places. David Buchan writes of a life and community spirit which has almost disappeared in the form he describes it, but those of us who have an abiding interest in the roots of our culture – the twee word might be heritage – owe him an immense debt for taking on the task of conveying his memories to print. His enthusiasm is such that the information spills out before the reader rather like a vast catch of herring slithering across the deck – rich, copious and unbridled. The book deserves to be widely read both in the North East and beyond.

John S. Smith
Director of the Centre for Scottish Studies
University of Aberdeen

Preface

To a you Buchan folkies
A scattered ower the world
I hope my Buchan stories
Remind you all of hame
And if you are a bittie young
And hinna seen the toonies
Then maybe jist, I can confirm
Your father's father's stories.

Your Granda may have been
A Lappie or a Soannie
Or maybe of anither sect
A Hocket, Pet or Lonnie
The Sanny Banks, the Kirky Brae
The Cample or the Shories
I'm sure you've heard it all before
From your father's father's stories.

The times were hard, the siller scarce
And money left the toonies
For foreign pairts or muckle toons
Tae make an honest penny.
Some of them did nae sae bad
And some did rather poorly
But most of them without a doubt
Passed on their fathers' stories.

And now they come from many pairts
Tae the Cample and the shories
Tae see the place their fathers left
And dwell upon his stories
Wi baggie packed and little cash
He went off in the trainie
It aa comes back though Dad's awa
But remembered for his stories.

The toonies meant a lot to Dad
He was a gie bit cannie lad
His stories were a bit outrageous
We said to him 'jist had yer tongue'
For you are jist a muckle le'er,
The're as true as I am livin'
That made him lach and lach sae sair
He was boo't twa faal upon the fleer.

But noo I've seen his little toonie
Though changed it has that certain feeling,
His cronnies are but memories now
As I walk with them along his shories
I know that he did want me
To see the toonie for myself
Not his mansions or his palaces
But jist his ain wee Butt an Ben.

The Village

I find that there are very few books dealing with Eastern Aberdeenshire and that those that do are brief in their dealings, particularly with the coastal Buchan villages. The village I intend to deal with is the village of St. Combs in Buchan.

The name Buchan is thought to be derived from the Latin *bos*, an ox.

Buchan land stretches from the river Ythan to the river Deveron. St. Combs is approximately five miles by road from Fraserburgh (The Broch). The twin villages of Inverallochy and Cairnbulg are in between, approximately three miles from Fraserburgh. The Aberdeen-Fraserburgh main road is the A92 and the Fraserburgh-Peterhead main road is the A952. The villages of St. Combs, Inverallochy and Cairnbulg are served by the B9033 off these main roads.

The original village of St. Combs was further inland than the present village, being located near the farm of Corskelly at Boatlea (Boatley). There is, now, no above ground trace of the old village (the auld toon). The fishermen in those days used the Boatlea shore for their fishing trips, launching and beaching their yawls by hand, assisted by their wives. From early records it appears that the inhabitants of Boatley were a pretty wild lot, as apparently an English boat ran aground nearby and the crew were subjected to very rough treatment.

From Church Records there were seven Buchans in the Boatley village. The auld kirk and school was considered to be not central enough and was moved to a sight where the old kirk and cemetery at Lonmay exists. At this time the church was complaining that there was a lot of bad money being put into the collection and it was even suggested that some were putting in bad money and taking out good.

There is some doubt about the origin of the name St. Combs but it is

1

thought to originate from the Christian missionary St. Colm, who travelled round the district, rather than from St. Columba of Iona and Abbey of Deer fame. The present village came into existence towards the end of the eighteenth century when it was thought that the periods of bad weather conditions, including sandstorms and cholera, were responsible for the creation of the new village (new toon). One of my distant forebears was one of the first settlers at the new site. The village is still known as 'new toon', especially by the folks of the neighbouring villages of Cairnbulg and Inverallochy.

St. Combs was made up of two parts, the separation being made by the Millburn. The northern part is known as Charleston, named after one of the lairds, Charles Fraser. This part is in the Parish of Rathen and is also nicknamed 'Sodom'. The larger southern part of the village is in the Parish of Lonmay. An early Laird, Charles Gordon, inherited the estate via his wife Jane. He died in 1796 and it was passed on to further Gordons. Cairness House was their home but the Gordons have now departed from the district and others occupy Cairness and the land is managed by another superior.

The Millburn enters the sea at the Millburn shore. It was crossed by an old timber bridge but this has been replaced by a concrete structure at the bottom of Bridge Street. There are two streets in the village named after the old Laird, namely Charles Street and Gordon Street. There were no Council houses in the early days and most of the houses were on what was called a 'Tenants at Will' basis. This meant that, although the occupiers had built the houses, the Laird had the overall rights to the property but, since the 1930 periods, the occupiers began to feu their properties and most are now fued or bought out. Council houses began to be erected in the thirties and there are now several streets of Council houses.

The village has only one vehicular entrance – this being on the Fraserburgh side of High Street. All the other streets run off High Street, mostly at right angles. The early street names before the advent of Council houses were as follows: Charleston ('Sodom'), High Street, Mid Street, East Street, Church Street, Charles Street, Gordon Street, West Street, Bridge Street, Braeheads. There were other houses which had no street names and were known by their house name only – there were: Seaview, Seafield, Lighthouse View and Vine Cottage. The Council houses which followed were Corskelly Place from the farm of Corskelly and West Park from West and Park District Councillors at the time of erection. There has now been considerable more Council building since the Second World War.

Mostly all the old style houses were built with their gable ends to the sea so as to minimise the effect of the salt-laden winds from the sea.

During my time in the village there would have been around 200 houses with a population of over 600. This varied a bit with the movement of people after the First World War, America claiming the most. There were no buildings of any significance in the village but the Hall (Kirky) in High Street, The School (High Street), The Auld School (High Street/Church Street), Mission Hall (Church Street), Butcher's (Church Street), Post Office and Shop (East Street), Dairy (Mid Street), Shoemaker (Dummy) (High Street), Bruce Shop (Gordon Street), Strachan Shop (Charles Street), Bruce Shop (West Street), 1. Buchan Shop (Mid Street), Buchan Shop (West Street), Buchan Dairy (Bridge Street), 2. Buchan Shop (Mid Street), Bakery (Charles Street), Station (West Street), were the most important.

The Butcher's shop was run by a family of Buchans who also had a shop in Inverallochy and Fraserburgh. The father was Peter Buchan (Butcher Patty) whose oldest son, Peter, was killed in a motor cycle accident at the Lumbs Road crossing. The second son, Butcher Alex, looked after the Fraserburgh and Inverallochy shops in conjunction with his father and assistants. Butcher Wullie looked after the St. Combs shop with assistance from William Buchan (Dan).

Practically all the other shops, as well as the Station, have disappeared or are under new ownership. The Post Office and East Street Shop were run by my father Patty, (Pet's Peter's Patty) but there will be greater detail of this later.

The Mission Hall (Bethel) was burnt down. Dairy Mid Street was managed by Margaret Buchan (Diry Marget), the milk coming from her father's farm at Cairnglass just outside the village. Several villagers used to hire a piece of land from Cairnglass and plant potatoes, which were collected during the tattie holidays. Bruce, West Street Shop, was owned by Wull, and his son carried on a joinery business at the rear of the shop. Wull used to run trips in a Model T Ford to Aberdeen, which was often a rather precarious journey. It was sometimes necessary to come out of the vehicle so that it could get up the brae at Ellon. He also had a country van round. Strachan, Charles Street Shop was run by Charlie and Lizickie but was a rather small shop. Strachan's Bakery was on the opposite side but closed and the family moved to New Pitsligo, where they opened a bakery shop and came to St. Combs with a van. My cousin stays there now. The shoemaker (Buchan, Dummy) closed down and moved to Aberdeen.

Shop West Street (Buchan – Jeanie Mannie) was a small shop run by cousins of ours. The daughter, Jessie Bella, was my 'Walk' partner, a second cousin. The brothers, John and James, were stalwarts in the St. Combs football team and both were joiners. Buchan Shop Mid Street (Banker Isie) was also a small house shop. A wooden addition was built on the west end of the house. This shoppie was important to us as she sold fireworks.

The other Mid Street Shop was owned by Jeannie Lonnie and was also a small shop in one end of the house. Bruce Shop, Gordon Street (Maggie Loves): her two sons Wulzie and John were also football stalwarts. John played for Fraserburgh and could have gone further if he had wished to move. They were my golfing companions to Fraserburgh Golf Course (Corbie).

Up until the 1930s the village had no properly surfaced road, High Street being the only hard surface. My father surfaced the road from High Street to our shop at 11 East Street, using 'danders' from the Station. There were no drains, no piped water, no proper sanitation, no Church, no ambulance, no policeman (an occasional visit from the policeman at Cairnbulg), no cars or lorries (until the late 1920s), no banks, no chemist, no pub or hotel, no doctor resident in the village (the nearest doctors were at Crimond or Fraserburgh), no minister or registrar (resident in the village), the nearest being at Lonmay.

The village, although classed as a fishing village, had no harbour, the yawls being launched and landed manually as in older times, again assisted by the women folk. There were several landing beaches, namely The Kittyloch, New Shore (Mid Point), St. Combs Haven (Mid Point), Cample (Southside). The Kittyloch (Kettyloch) was used mostly by the Charleston yawls.

One attribute the village has is its miles of golden sands, the beach stretching from the Cample to Rattray Head. The sea bathing is also very safe and the uncrowded links is suitable for camping, the bents and links being ideal for children.

There has been a bit of inter-marriage between the three villages of St. Combs, Inverallochy and Cairnbulg. Any St. Combs lad courting a girl from the other villages used to speak about 'going ower tae wheelick' tae see his blon'.

The villages of Inverallochy and Cairnbulg are separated by a small stream (The Stripe) and it is very difficult for a visitor to locate the dividing line, but the locals will soon make you aware whether they are 'Bulgers' or 'Cotoners'. The St. Combers know the Inverallochy folk as

'Cotoners' as the village was known as the Cot-town, whilst the folk from Cairnbulg were known as Bulgers or Bilgers. St. Combs inhabitants are known as New Tooners or Quities (Quities, Goonies and Tailies).

From what has gone before, it can be seen that Buchans, Bruces and Strachans are the predominant names in St. Combs and, unless a nickname is used, it is very difficult to pinpoint a particular person.

A Walk Along the Line

When he gid ower tae Bilger toon
Tae see his Bilger lass
He aye gid by the line
It was drier than the grass
He steppit on the sleepers
But sometimes they were slippy
Expecially if there wis a shewer
O rain or sna or sleet
This time there were three of them
Aa on the same design
Tae ging ower the line
To see their lass in Wheelick.
An as they newsd on their steppin
Twas een ahin the ither
As Charlie turned his heid aroon
Tae speak tae his pal John
His tae it took the line side on
And he landed in a heep
His face it got a gie bit knock
And he quidna mak his feet
His pals they found he'd broken his queet
An they tied his twa legs thegither
Wi hankies and wi bits o' cloot
And carrit him as best they could
To his hame among the quities
Nae Bilger quines for him again
Twas a visit fae the doctor
When he wis teen tae Aberdeen
Tae get his leggie set
It was then pit in plaister.
Nae mair trips tae Bilger toon

By stepping along the sleepers
In fact he never walked that way again
But merrit a quine doon Sooth

The following are some of the nicknames that have been used over the last hundred years or so.

A. Adie, Annicky, Ackie, Aggie.
B. Beedie, Billicky, Bilshie, Baab, Beelder, Beedicky, Bulfer, Buck, Benshie, Binsil, Bowdy, Bide, Boxy, Banker, Buckie, Bird, Breece, Breecy, Bougie, Blow, Barber, Baker, Bumble, Buzz, Bowfie, Beena, Becka, Bo.
C. Catta, Coty, Cowkie, Cly, Chumphy, Choppy, Coxen, Cha, Creepin Eevie, Corky, Cookie, Craw
D. Dannels, Dodicky, Deericks, Dag, Daisy, Dicky, Duncan, Dyle, Dan, Dowd, Davicky, Duth, Dooey, Dummy, Dites, Doh.
E. Eppy, Easie, Embo, Ellie, Eh-nae, Eateo.
F. Fadry, Fitie, Fleppy, Fite, Freendy.
G. Gaggers, Gamrie, Greevy, Gick, Gay, Gran, Gena, Gibb.
H. Hock, Hocket, Hacket, Hap, Hope, Hog, Hunnert, Hun.
I. Isicky, Isie, Isibellicky.
J. Jum, Jimky, Jonsie, Jap, Jute, Jo, Jeemsie, Jot.
K. King, Kingie, Kirky, Kaiser.
L. London, Lizicky, Lammie, Lap, Ludo, Luggies, Lonnie, Leeby.
M. Mugsie, Magsy, Magity, Mash, Micick, Master, Mannie, Muff, Mull, Maisy, Mattie, Miney.
N. Non, Nonter, Nicka, Nip, Nellsie.
O. Onack, Officer, Onzie, Onnie, Organ.
P. Putler, Puldy, Perky, Pyme, Pug, Pum, Pret, Pet, Poker, Poddick.
Q. Quarrie, Quik-wash, Quinn.
R. Rotty, Running, Rogue.
S. Shoddy, Sanick, Shaver, Shoug, Spunky, Spotty, Sheelicks, Scoot, Sun, Soan, Soay, Stoot, Suffie.
T. Talla, Tan, Tonner, Tilt, Tandick, Tachy, Torry, Toll, Toppy, Tarry, Titt, Toe.
U. Uncle.
V. Vester.
W. Wast, Wulzie, Wulty, Wye, Wiver, Woordly, Wullicky, Wakey, Wull, Wudd.
X. Xmas Charlie.

Y. Yank, Ya-hoo.
Z. Zander, Zak.

The nicknames often bear no relationship to either their surnames or Christian names. Some names may refer to the person's job, such as: Barber Jimmy, Baker Andy, Butcher Alex, Diry (Dairy) Margaret, Coal Tom, Post Office Patty. Some names were passed from father to son – William Buchan (Daisy) whose son was Daisy's Andra, who later became Daisy when his father died. William Buchan (Dan) – his son became Dan when his father died. There were some double and treble names. For example: Hocket begat Hocket's Wullie, who begat Hocket's Wullie's Jeemsie. My father was Pet's Peter's Patty, who later became Patty, and I was known as Patty's David, not as Pet's Peter's Patty's David. Another triple was Hock's Andy's Jeck. Some doubles were: Onack's Mary – Onack's Davie; Nicka's Wulzie – Nicka's Helen; Tonner's Jimmy – Ton's Pat – Jeannie Lonnie – Putler's Bill – Torry Dody – Nellsie Annie – Jean Jo – Tan's John – Lappy's Andra – Mugsie's Maggie – Andra Perky – Duncan's Alex – Leeby Gick – Jeemsie Wye – Peter Spotty – Fleppie's Andra – Wull's John – Dag's Sandy – Shougie's Andra. There were brothers and sisters among the foregoing and they could use their fathers' by-names. For example: Duncan's Pat, Duncan's Nan, Johnnie Lonnie, Aggie Gick, John Gick.

Some names were taken from either the maternal or paternal side, i.e. Daisy and Magity married, their eldest son became Daisy's Andra, the second son was always known as Puldy, whilst the third son was known as Magity's Dody, whilst the daughter was known as Jeannie Love. Polly (Grannie Polly Bruce) handed down her name to her offspring, Polly's Joe, Polly's Andra, Polly's Kirsten, Polly's Mary. Some of the incomers who married St. Combs' people might retain the names of their place of birth, i.e. Gamrie Leeby – she came from Gardenstown (Gamrie); Embo Bella (from Embo).

Some even dropped their long-winded nicknames and acquired new names. Hocket's Wullie's Jeemsie became Bumble and his sons were known as Bumble's Jim and Bumble's Wellum and his daughter was always known as Leeby Ann. Cowkie's Jim became Toll, Sun's Tom became Coal Tom, Nellsie's Annie (cripple Annie) became Teuchet.

These are just a few of the nicknames that were used, some local school nicknames which had a short life and some which died out through lack of usage; not only the Buchans, Bruces, etc., had tee names. Some of the newer names like Walker Jack had nicknames. The Walkers had a Craw and Spicey and the Jacks had Bird, Bean, Shaver; Forman – Kingie; Nicol – Jot and Peat; Stephen – Fadry and Sheelicks; Stephen-Toe – Bobby Toe and Alicky Toe.

Gemmie Jessie, her husband was a gamekeeper on the local estate and retired to St. Combs. Their name was Murdoch. Some people had two names, ie. Mr. Strachan was known as Non and Growge.

J. Buchan – Johan's Johnny and Stylie, and his brother Sandy was known as Johan's Sandy (maternal side), also as Sandy Mackie (paternal side), his father was known as Mackie or John Gick.

John Bruce (Annie Cummin's Johnny) left the fishing and bought the farm of Middleton and became Johnnie Middleton. Charles Bruce (Johnnie Breecy's Charlie) bought the farm Den O'Howie and became Den O'Howie. One person in the other village became 7½ – his house number – whilst another became V.C. Joe for his V.C. decoration.

Another was known as Christmas Charlie as during the Yarmouth fishing he came home at Christmas time, about a month after the other boats. Patty's oldest son was named Sylvester, after one of the travellers that visited the shop; this was shortened to Vester by the villagers but when he started work in the Post Office he was known as Sylvie, his son Sylvester being known as Vester.

The Village Ode

A long time ago a gale arose
It blew and blew for days on end
It lifted sand fae miles aroon
And happit up St. Combs.

They howkit oot a new St. Combs
A mile or twa awa
And then the biggit hooses
Wi muckle steens and clay.

The demon drink it was a curse
With cholera too, t'was even worse
The folkies blamed the wrath of God
That's why, they left for pastures new.

All that my freens, noo far away
Nae hooses noo, are built wi' clay

So think again before ye pine
For these old days of auld lang syne

This is what we like to believe, historians may say otherwise.

School Days

My first memories of St. Combs were when I was about three years old. I was carried down to the beach (the sanny banks) by my father. There was quite a few people there, gazing out to sea with spy-glasses and telescopes as apparently a German submarine had been sighted and reported to the authorities by my father, and shortly afterwards a British warship appeared on the horizon; what the outcome was, I am not sure.
Another episode was the crashing of a seaplane near the Loch of Strathbeg. The Loch was used for Seaplanes during the First World War. There were many trophy hunters collecting pieces of the abandoned plane. I had a small wheel which I kept for years but it was lost sometime during my many shifts. There was also an airship base at Lenabo, near Mintlaw.
On reaching the age of five I went to the local Primary School. I was pleased to attend the school but was rather disappointed I couldn't walk out when I liked. The teacher for us newcomers was a Miss Henderson from the Kininmonth District. She was a very good, kind and patient teacher. I remember her as a nice neat and tidy lady, her hair done up in a bun, and usually she wore a white blouse and skirt. She also had a large wart on her right cheek. Another memory I had of her was when she gave me half a crown (12½p.) as a prize for a crayon drawing of forget-me-nots which had been submitted to a children's exhibition. These were the days of the tawse and strap but I can't remember receiving any punishments from Miss Henderson. During the week she stayed in digs with Mrs. Cow (San's Cow's wife) at 4 Mid Street and, weather permitting, she cycled home to Kininmonth at the weekend. She left the village to teach in the local school at Kininmonth and the children were sorry to see her go. Sometime after she left I met her at Denhead Stores and she recognised me right away and enquired about all my old classmates, naming them in

10

School class, 1911.

Public School, St. Combs.

turn and asking about all the folkies she knew in St. Combs and asking me to send her kind regards. She was followed by a Miss Milne, who stayed with Mrs. Cheyne at 4 High Street.

On our first year or so we used skalie and sklate for our lessons (slate and slate pencil). These writing utensils, like school children's respect for their teachers, are a thing of the past. I still remember some of the stories from my primary class books: *The Chinaman and the Toboggan* – 'Me wanty no swish swish walky back a mile'; *The General and the Corporal* – 'Heave O, cried the Corporal, but would not lend a hand himself'; *The Robin in the Barn*'; etc. The school games we played during our stint with Miss Henderson were 'Ring-a-Ring of Roses' – 'The farmer's in his dell' – 'The Grand old Duke of York' – 'There was a jolly miller' – 'The good ship sails through the ally ally O' – 'I sent a letter to my love' – 'Here we go round the Mulberry Bush'. Some of my classmates then were: A. Buchan (Save), Wm. Buchan (Dan), I. Buchan (Jessie Bella), G. Buchan (Gena), Peter Buchan (Peter Buzz), my inseparable pal, J. Hendry (Tonguee), John Strachan (Johnny eh nae), John Buchan (Baab), John Cow (Micick). Others in the classes above were Scott Cranna, Wull's John, Maggie Bidey, Soay's Isabella, Stoot, Alex Walker, etc. A few of those in the class below were Law Cranna, Andra Perky, Mugsie's Maggie, London's Betsy, etc. After our term with Miss Henderson we then left the sklates, etc., and passed through the dividing doors to Miss Buchan (Leeby Cook), a local girl; she was Cook's daughter and stayed at 5 Church Street. Her sister Kirsten went to New Zealand and Leeby followed later; her brother Cookie went to the herring fishing. My recollection of Leeby Cook was that she was always prancing and preeming and fiddling with her dress. Another time we heard that she was going to Aberdeen to get a PERMANENT WAVE (a rarity in those days) and on Monday morning all eyes were agog to see what miracles had been carried out on Miss Buchan's head. I think we expected her to appear with the crown jewels, for we were all rather disappointed at the outcome.

From Miss Buchan, we passed onto the Headmaster's room, Mr. Mcleod (from Lewis). He was known as 'Ginger', for he was supposed to be grey haired but was reputed to have dyed his hair. He always appeared to be under strain for, apart from having a son, he had a daughter who didn't keep very well and his wife had died earlier. When he retired he went to live in Aberdeen in a boarding house in Springbank, which a St. Combs family had opened (the Ritchie Family). The pupils stayed with Mr. McLeod until they passed their qualifying exam and went to the Fraserburgh Academy, or stayed on until they were fourteen and left for

A St. Combs School class, 1916.

the outside world. In those days if we had seen the Headmaster outwith the school we made ourselves scarce. If we got any thrashings for misdeeds, it was kept very quiet for, if our parents got to know, more than likely we would have got another dose. Visits by parents to chastise teachers were unknown in these days. I got a few hidings from 'Ginger' for such things as climbing on the roof, dodging to herd cattle from the station.

The games we played at this time were Han (Hand) panning. This we used to do in the shelter sheds. A hole was made about two feet from the floor in the back wall of the shed. The boys raced towards this hole, would place their toe in the hole and jump up to catch the roof joists, then swing across these joists like apes to see who could make the most crossings. We also played all the usual playground games, but for football and cricket we adjourned to the park behind the 'Kirky', being recalled by the school hand bell. This park is now built upon with Council houses (Corskelly Place). We knew it as the little perky. It was over the dyke from the Cranna's house. There were so many Buchans at the school at this time that two or three teams of Buchans could be formed.

Goalkeepers   John Buchan (Cly's Johnnie)
                 Andrew Buchan (Shougie's Andra)
                 John Buchan (Tan's John)

Backs   Andrew Buchan (Fleppy's Andra)
                 James Buchan (Cly's James)
                 A. Buchan (Sandy Bide)
                 Wm. Buchan (Dan)

Halves   Ernest Buchan (Johan's Ernest)
                 Sandy Buchan (Sandy Mackie)
                 J. Buchan (Johnny Bide)
                 D. Buchan (Patty's David)
                 J. Buchan (Brucie's John)
                 A. Buchan (Duncan's Alex)
                 Peter Buchan (Peter Spotty)
                 J. Buchan (Johnnie Lonnie)

Forwards   J. Buchan (Johan's Johnny)
                 S. Buchan (Patty's Vester)
                 P. Buchan (Peter Buzz)
                 A. Buchan (Brucie's Sandy)
                 A. Buchan (Andra Perky)
                 A. Buchan (Stoot)
                 J. Buchan (Baab)
                 J. Buchan (Darkie Jim)

Several more Buchans could be added to this list for practically everyone in the village played football at one time or another. Matches in a summer evening could reach twenty a side. Players just arrived at the pitch and joined in. When we were too young to participate in the big matches we played on what was known as the little pitchy at the back of the old cemetery. The original pitch was at a flat piece of ground not far from the Tillyduff and the team played in green tops and white shorts. The new pitch was located in the park in front of the houses at 'Seaview' – 'Seafield'.

As bairns our pants were made from a floorbag which was well bleached. The football was obtained by collected cards from packets of soap, or collecting threepence from members of the team – a football costing 5s. 0d. (five shillings) (25p). With the addition of a few other names like Bruce, Cranna, Strachan, Cheyne, etc., quite a good team could be produced.

The rivalry between the various villages was pretty hectic and if you won away from home you had to make a quick exit with your bike if your tyres had not been let down. Some players from the village teams went on to play in Highland League Football and some could have gone further if they had wished to do so. One that did aspire to greater things was Andy Cheyne, who went on to play for Glasgow Rangers and gain medals in the process. Toxy went to Rochdale. At one time we had a goalkeeper named Skinner who had no feet and had artificial metal supports and feet. I remember once while playing one of the bolts snapped and he was left with one foot and a stump. Skinner stumped about in goal while a young lad was sent to his house to fetch a new foot and a spanner.

On reaching the age of eleven the St. Combs pupils who had qualified, and who wished to go, went to the Fraserburgh Academy whilst the remainder stayed on with the Headmaster until they reached the age of fourteen. Those that left for the Academy during my year were Jessie Bella (J. Buchan), Gena Buchan (G. Buchan) Jimmy Hendry (Tonguee) and myself. Others that followed were Peter Buchan (Peter Buzz), A. Buchan (Perky's Andra) and Lawrence Cranna, etc. The Headmaster at the Academy during my time was Daddy Lees; he stayed in King Edward Street and usually cycled to his work straight backed and wearing a bowler hat. He was an austere individual, very unapproachable and one of the old school. One particular memory of him was when my chum (Jimmy Noble) and I were dragged from the morning assembly hall prayers and pushed into his room. We were supposed to have been creating a disturbance. We, of course, pled 'not guilty' but, as was expected, our pleas were rejected and we both got six of the best. That was the old style of doing things: guilty or not somebody had to be made an example. My arms bore the marks for some time and I had to be careful not to let my parents see the marks or it would most certainly have been another censure.

The Academy teachers during my terms were Mr. Forbes (Head Maths), Mr. Smart (Head English), Mr. Lipp (Head Science), Mr. Munro (Head Art), Miss Ewan (Head French), Mr. Gavin (Head Latin), Mr. Burnett (Crafts), Mr. Cordiner (English), Miss Bain (English), Miss Elder (Latin), Miss Watt (Maths), Miss McAlpine (French), another Miss Ewen (French), Mr. Johnstone (English), Miss Grant (English). There was a music teacher and physical instructor. I received the tawse from a few of them and lots of impositions as well. If we had been dodging a period we used to wait in the outside toilets until we heard the period bell and then rejoin the class for the next period. Most of the dodging was done to play billiards or snooker in a small shop/café in College Bounds. At that time it cost threepence for half an hour. Also, if the rocket went off for the lifeboat to be launched, we were away down to the harbour. I can recall an incident in the toilets whilst I was dodging Latin. This lad came into the toilets and inserted a squib (banger) into the flushing hole of the toilet. This usually gave a loud bang when the banger exploded, but unfortunately this time it blew the whole toilet to bits. The whole lot of us bolted over the dyke and made a quick exit. An investigation followed but the culprit was never found. The young lad kept on at us not to tell anyone, which we never did.

Unfortunately for us St. Combs pupils who used to take our lunch sandwiches in the school, we were now debarred from the school and we had to adjourn to a café where we got soup and pudding for a sixpence. At the eleven o'clock break the baker's and ice cream barrows used to wait outside the school gates. The usual break was a cinnamon roll (halfpenny) and ice cream (halfpenny). The aforesaid wall also played a part in the introduction of all new boy pupils. The field over the dyke was grazed by cows who usually left their trademarks behind the wall. On the day the school opened all the young boys were pushed over the wall and reaped the consequences, that is, until one lad had his arm broken and then this stupid practice was stopped.

Very few St. Combs pupils in my year reached any great academic heights, although some before and quite a few later went on to University. There are a few who come to mind: *Doctors*: Davie West, W. Bruce (Breecy), A. Buchan (Bruce's Sandy), George Bruce (Polly Joe's George); *Teachers*: A. Bruce (Polly's Andra), A. Cow (Sandy Miller), John Duthie (John Mull). It has now become ordinary for the St. Combs pupils to reach University standard, qualifications in all the arts and sciences becoming commonplace.

I left the Academy in the fourth year with no misgivings and went on to qualify as a wireless operator, but this was during the depression and I couldn't find a job. I did odd jobs about my father's shop and post office, including driving the car for hire. In 1935 I joined the Post Office Engineering Department and spent forty years in various parts of the U.K., finishing as an Executive Engineer in Aberdeen where I retired in 1976. Shortly after I joined the Post Office, I got a call to join the Merchant Shipping as a Marconi Operator, I declined, which may have been a wise move for many of my ex-wireless friends were killed during the Second

World War. When my father was killed in 1938, my mother asked if I wanted to take over the shop and Post Office but I declined as, even at that time, the demise of the small shop was in the offing, with the advent of travelling vans; but even these were being killed by the large market stores.

And so it was goodbye to the Academy. During my time there, I always felt that the teachers were less than generous to the less intellectual pupils and tended to belittle the village pupils. The teachers', ministers' and doctors' sons and daughters were the favourites. This was further brought out to me by one of my pals, who transferred to Peterhead Academy as he had shifted house to Mintlaw. He told me it was like a different world; instead of being one of the duffers, he was treated differently and became one of the brighter students and he enjoyed his time there.

One incident that sticks in my mind from the Academy is that during my school days I suffered from asthma (my maternal grandfather and uncles were also troubled) and during my last year I was off school for a while and fell behind, especially in English. I had done fairly well the previous terms. When I came back this teacher put the whole class in a line with me at the top. He then plied me with questions from parts which I had missed, until I had landed at the bottom which seemed to give him great satisfaction. After that I was completely lost and couldn't get away from the school fast enough.

During my earlier days in the Post Office, I worked both in Peterhead and Fraserburgh and found that the attitude to the fisher folk in Peterhead is so different to that of Fraserburgh. Perhaps it has changed since my time. I remember a conversation my father had with a visitor to the shop. He asked him what he thought about the two towns. He replied that he thought the Brochers were trying to ape Piccadilly and if you don't understand this it's simply that they are trying to be something which they are not. Even today Peterhead has expanded much more than the Broch, Peterhead being the largest fish market in the U.K. and it has also acquired more from the oil. There is rivalry between Fraserburgh and Peterhead just as there is between the villages, especially the football teams. My wife is a 'blue toon' fisherman's daughter and a bonny lassie she was. Her father was Alex Duthie, skipper of the family drifter *Protect me*. On his death the elder son, Robert, skippered the boat. Another son, Alex, was also on the drifter.

The School

When I was five or thereabouts
I hid to ging tae skweel
I got my baggie and my sklate
My screechin skalie tee
But best of all my playtime piece
A saftie wi some jam.

The wifie wi her hair deen up
She met us at the door
And said, 'Now children follow me',
And led us a inside
And as she shut the door on us
Wee Johnny was needin to pee.

The teacher said, 'Now Johnny lad,
Why didn't you go before?'
'Weel, wifie, fou wis I tae ken
That you would shut the door?
At hame I just can please maesel
And ging oot when I like.'

The first day it was a sae strange
The neist nae muckle better
But before ye kent, it was part of life
Wi beuks and sums and spellin
And soon we left oor ain wee skweel
To earn oorsels a crust o breed

An on through life its troubled ways
Why some got mair than ithers
Some have kept the straight and narrow
Whilst others have geen tae gite
But ae thing sure, we'll a mine on
It's oor ain wee couthie skweelie.

The Loonie's Hoast

Her loonie he came doon the stairs
Wi an awfa makkin-on hoast
And as he hid his brakfist
Said 'Mam I canna ging tae skweel,
Jist listen tae ma hoast'
Aricht mi loon I'll see fit I can dee
And fae the press she took oot
That bottle o' castor oil
Oh no Mam, yer coorse tae me
Castor Oil is nae for hoasts
It's for a sair belly
Granny aye gies tae me a honey drink
Wi' a gravet roon mi neck.
Na mi loon jist tak yer baggie
And here's yer playtime piece
At denner time he rushed in
And sat down at the table
The castor oil was sitting there
Beside his plate o' soup
He pushed it roon ahin the loaf
Syne supped his soup and raisined rise
And finished aff wi tae and snappies
He wis oot the door in a flash
Wi' nae a ward o hoast,
The neist day it was Setterday
Fin it wis strips and fitba beets
And he came hame jist clartit
But fit aboot that naesty hoast
And jist far hid it geen
It must have been that awfa bottle
Hid a genie corkit in't.

After School

There was very little organised entertainment in the village, so that children and teenagers had to organise most of their own games and pranks. One such prank we used to play was what was called Dirlin Windows. This involved getting an empty cotton reel (a pirn) and notching the edges with a knife; a rounded piece of wood around nine inches long was pushed through the hole, then a piece of string about a yard long was wrapped round the reel. The reel was then placed against the window pane and the string given a strong pull. This gave a loud rasping noise which startled the occupants and usually resulted in a chase. This device was known as a 'dirler'.

Another somewhat similar device was known as a 'Titler'. This consisted of a string – say, ten to fifteen yards long – enough to get you a hiding place. A pin was attached to the distant end of the string and, at a distance of about a foot from the pin, a small pebble or some other suitable weight was attached. The pin was then pushed into the window woodwork so that the weight dangled against the window pane. From our hidden position, the far end of the string was pulled and slackened and this caused the weight to rattle against the window. Again this would result in being chased.

Still another caper used was what was called 'fummen the spoots'. An old piece of newspaper was rolled lengthwise, this was then pushed up the downpipe of the guttering and set alight. This would cause a roaring noise and again we would be chased.

Some of the houses in the village were rather low, so that it was fairly easy to reach the lum (chimney) and we used to climb up and place a sod on top of the lum (Kirsten Mannies was one such hoosie). There was usually only one door to the house and this was barred by tying the sneck

20

(latch) to a pole placed across the doorway. The house became full of smoke and this resulted in the fire having to be put out and the windows opened.

Still another trick was to parcel up a load of rubbish in a box and deliver it to a house and, as there were no lights in the village, the deliverer was not seen. Another prank was to obtain an old empty syrup tin (there were usually plenty lying on the beach), pierce a small hole in the side of the tin about half an inch from the bottom, and put carbide and a little water in the tin, then push the lid home. When it was thought that sufficient gas had been generated, a lighted match was put to the small hole; this caused an explosion and the lid was blown off.

In a somewhat similar vein, another prank was to get a strong lemonade bottle and put in some carbide and water. A cork was inserted in the top and when enough gas had been generated, this blew the cork out. Carbide was readily available as bicycle lamps were lit by gas, having superseded oil lamps. A tin of carbide cost sixpence. Gas was later replaced by electric battery cycle lamps. There were very few fruit trees or fruit as the salt-laden winds would have damaged them and, if they survived the winds, they didn't survive the loons. The farmers' fields would be raided for swedes, which would be cut open and scraped with a mussel shell and eaten that way. Peas, tares and locust beans were also available in the fields (locust beans were fed to sheep). During the Hogmanay and New Year period, depredation of one kind or another was carried out and all sensible persons would put all moveable objects under lock and key. Even then, such items as poles, gates, toilets, yawls would be displaced and this meant owners hunting around the village for lost property. There were other tricks the lads got up to but they never seemed to come to any harm or result in repercussions. I can't remember any police action being taken.

Some of the older boys would make home-made boats with hoops and canvas, tarring the whole assembly several times. Providing the weather was fine, the canvas boats would be used for fishing. Mrs. Trail's sons had a boat which they stored in St. Combs and used it for sea trips. It was called the *Cowbel* (Cobble). The Brick Wally loch and Calders loch froze over during the winter months and with 'tackety beets' we used them for sliding (skating). With a coat raised above our heads like a sail, we used to take a long run/jump on the ice and were blown at great speed across the ice. Slides were also formed on the village braes, like High Street. Sledges were homemade and used on the village or links braes. Many a window was broken by snowball fights.

After School

The school it closed at fower o'clock
The cleaner came near five
There wisna muckle time for us
To get oor playtime ba
It was kicket up upon the reef
And we man get it doon

Now Peet and I climbed up the pipes
An along the gutters tee
Syne ower the sklates tae the riggin-tile
And down the valley called sin
There wis oor ba and ither twa
And lots of ither things

There wis a beet, a mitten tee
A beuk, a sklate, a tin
A bonnet wi a toorie on
An auld and wizened craw
And doon we threw the useful things
And hurried back to claim them

And we were jist in time me lads
For at the gate, there 'Ginger' stood
The cleaner and a dog
We scampered through the playground
An ower the dyke at Wulls
The booty in oor pooches a fortune tae us loons.

I didna think that we were seen
By the 'Ginger' or the 'Jannie'
But come next day, it was seen
The mannie seemed affa happy
Come Buchan D. and Buchan P.
And he gave us a lickin

In spite of all his trials and strife
He wis a kindly crater
We didna maybe think so then

But bairnies didn't think
If we had life to live again
Maybe we would do it better.

Games and Entertainment

This is an enlargement on the previous chapter.

One of the most common kids' games were girds (hoops) and this entailed a visit to Forsyth's smiddy just outside the village where, for a few pence, you got a gird. A cleek (pusher) was made from a piece of fencing wire formed to a U-shape, the driving end, and a handle was formed at the other end. The girds would be propelled along with the cleeks racing each other along the roads, often bumping your fellow girders' hoops over. Sometimes a stick was used as the driving force.

Bools (marbles) was another common game. There were various types of marbles and various types of games. The largest type of bool we used was called a canon and was slightly less in size than a golfball. The next size was named a bool and was about three quarters of an inch in diameter. Some of them had acquired a reddish tint in the firing process and these were called 'reed cheekers'. Glessers were made of glass and had various patterns and colours in their make-up. Steelers were obtained from the ball races of old discarded cars or lorries. The small coloured ones we called donners. The values were two donners to a bool and two bools to a canon. The various games played with bools were Ringie, Kypie, pitching and spanning. In spanning the lads with the big hands had the advantage as you had to span between the bools to win your reward of a donner.

A game played on the links was called 'Soddy' or 'Knifie'. This involved cutting a circle in the turf with a bullseye in the centre. The game was played with knives in a similar manner to darts. The outer ring was ten, the bullseye twenty and the part in between five. Each lad would throw the knives and the last one to reach the agreed total was sodded. He had to run a distance of approximately twenty yards and return to the circle, being pelted with sods by the other players during his run.

A dangerous game we used to play was to obtain an old vehicle tyre, curl up inside and roll down a brae such as the Tillyduff or Brick Wall Brae. It was surprising no one came to harm.

Bull the cuddy was played and this was a modified version of leap frog. A boy stood upright and another boy went down touching the upright boy; then in leap frog fashion you leapt on to the bent lad, the bent boys were gradually increased and the others leapt on to the assembly until the whole lot collapsed.

Other games

Turn the cat or helster gowdie (head over heels) on the links.

Tackie, Coupin the ladle (see-saw). The see-saws were made by using a mason's meer (trestles) and a builder's batten, usually obtained from the builder's yard.

Huns (hounds) and hares. This consisted of forming sides, the hounds chasing the hares all round the village until all were caught. Cowboys and Indians and hoist the green flag were played on a similar basis to the foregoing. Bows and arrows, the arrows being made from a cane or a whittled piece of stick with a nail in front: the bows were made from the hoops used to make the trunks (creels) used for crab fishing.

Slings and catapults. Slings would be made from old boots and catapults from an old car tube.

Can walking. Old syrup tins were used. Two holes were punched in the bottom, string was threaded through the holes and loops formed. The loops were held in the hands and feet were placed on the tins and you walked along standing on the tins. Stilts were also used but the walking was on a much higher level. Scrap wood from the beach or old clothes poles were used to make the stilts.

Draygons (kites) and darkies (another form of kite) were also made from willow cane or whittled sticks, with the addition of string paper, thread or paste. The flying string was usually from an old fishing line or mending cotton, the tails were made from an old piece of herring net. The Sanny Banks was the favourite place for kite flying as the strong sea breezes gave the kites a lift.

Home peeries (tops), home-made whistles and pea shooters made from a weed we called 'kicks'. We also made soapy bubbles from soap powder and used an old clay pipe to blow the bubbles. The bubbles were made more durable by adding a little glycerine.

Caps (keps) were brought in little penny boxes and these were exploded between two metal domes attached to string.

Cigarette card collecting from cigarette packets or from sweet packets or soap cartons. Sets of footballers, cricketers, cries of London, flowers, etc., etc. Also transfers (scraps) and these we wet and stuck on our hands or school books. These sold for one penny a sheet (two dozen).

Catching seagulls was another ploy. A few hooks were attached to stones and baited with fish livers or herring. The gulls would swoop down and get their beaks caught in the hook. After playing about with the gulls for a while and getting a few pecks in the process, we usually marked the gulls with something on their legs and then released them; when they appeared to be none the worse, you could catch the same one again.

Bird nesting, especially craws' eggs, was another seasonal pastime. Round about the beginning of April when the Easter holidays were on the go, we would go up to the craw wud (wood) for the afternoon. On the way up we would call into the country shop (Gowanhill) and purchase a pennyworth of broken biscuits. This consisted of brown and white ginger biscuits, coconut, farthings and rice. Other items could be purchased for a one half penny or one penny.

If a bicycle wasn't available, we walked all the way to the woods. We were never able to have a bike for everyone. We would perhaps have a bike between four of us so what we did was called 'spellin'. Two of us would use the bike, one driving the other on the cycle bar or back step. We proceeded along the road for a few hundred yards and left the bike at the side of the road within sight of the other two, who walked on to pick up the bike and proceed in a similar manner as the first two. The first two would be walking on and would be overtaken and passed by the second pair, who went on for a few hundred yards and left the bike as before. This relief method was used until we reached our destination, thus saving a little time. A similar method was used on our return journey but with the added weight of a few dozen eggs. The trees where the craws nested must have been well over thirty feet high and the lower ten to fifteen feet were fairly short of branches, so we had to scramble up gripping the trunk with our legs and arms. After we reached the tree limbs it was much easier to climb. All this time the craws would be creating a terrible din, squawking their heads off. On reaching the top of the tree it was like an island with nests in abundance. The greedy craws used to pinch others' eggs and young birds to feed their own brood. It was pandemonium when we showed our heads above the tree top. The gathering of eggs was a simple matter and these we lowered down to our partners at the bottom. We tested the eggs in a burn, and if the eggs sank they were fresh and if they floated they were rotten. Craw eggs weren't so good as plover eggs (teuchets). In spite of all our raiding of the craws' nests, the population never seemed to decrease as there always seemed to be as many the next year.

The Loch of Strathbeg was another venture ground where we gathered tern, coot, water hen, duck and other species' eggs, but regulations were brought in which put a stop to bird nesting.

Another ploy was the snaring of small birds on the nearby farms like Bankhead (Bankies). Our aim was to catch linnets or red-breasted sparrows, which were used as songbirds or crossed with canaries, a Border or Norwich. Some reckoned they got a better song from a cross. The method we used to trap the birds is described as follows. We covered a gird with herring fish net, securing it to the hoop sides with string. The hoop was then propped up with a piece of stick about twelve to fifteen inches long, a long piece of string was attached to the stick (we hid behind a haystack). Bait in the form of seeds or crumbs was laid below the hoop contraption, and when the birds were pecking away, we pulled the string removing the stick and the hoop fell on top of the birds without harming them. Sometimes a riddle was used.

The village being on the coast, it was natural that all types of fishing were popular. Setting shore lines was used a lot until the thirties, when inshore trawling swept up most of the fish we would have caught. For a shore line, a discarded piece of small line (smallin) from one of the yawls was used. This line was stretched out on the sand at low water (when the tide was out). It was anchored by digging in stones at its end and in between. The line was pushed into the sand by a graip (digging fork), leaving only the tippens (twisted horse hair) and hooks visible. The hooks were baited with sand eels (sannel), lug (lugworm) or herring. We used to stand by waiting until the line was covered by the rising tide to chase the gulls away. We were usually digging for sannel or lug at this time. Our catches were flounders, freshwaters, sea trout, saithe, cod, etc.

Hand line (hanlin) from the many deep pools in the area (The Loup), New Shore, The Pot and from the yawls which we sometimes borrowed. Fishing off Rattray Head could produce some lovely cod from this type of fishing. The bait we used on the hand line were soft crab bait (pillers and peels). Rattray Head was a very dangerous place to fish. You had to watch the tide and weather carefully as, with only a sail and oars, you could be swept round the head if you weren't careful. You had to be away before the tide turned. Us lads used to search the rocks and seaweed for the crab bait. We tested to see if the crabs were mature enough by breaking off one of the tips of the small toes. The right type could get a halfpenny or one penny from Johnny Breecy. Johnny Breecy was the first one to have a motor-driven yawl. He visited a son in America and brought home an outboard motor.

When you were baiting your hand line hook with a piller or peel, you had to wrap it round with some sheep's wool as this made it more durable, preventing the fish from cleaning it up at the first go. I remember once, while out on a trip to Rattray Head with my Uncle Sandy and cousin Cha, I must have been using an old line, for when I was dragging in this line, I was just about to pull this monster cod aboard when the hook came off. I wasn't believed and was said to have caught the bottom of the pot hole. However, when Johnny Breecy, who was fishing nearby, came home he said he had caught a monster cod with a hook in its mouth.

A 'Sappus' was a device we used to catch crabs. An old piece of herring netting was filled with fish heads and lowered into a rock pool. The crabs and lobsters came out and attached themselves to this and we then pulled in the device and took off the crabs. Gathering whelks was another pastime and these we gathered from rock pools and seaweed. They were gathered in tins and pails, packed in a hessian bag with some seaweed, and put on the trainee for the South Market. If they arrived fresh, we would perhaps receive the princely sum of 5/- (25p.) but sometimes a letter would arrive stating 'consignment received, dead and dying'; this applied particularly to lobsters and crabs. Consignments of crabs and lobsters were sent south packed in crates. These crabs were caught in what were locally called trunks (creels); most other places around the coast called them creels.

Sailing segs (broad grassies), paper boats, made from old jotters and sailed in the Cat Loch, Little Potty or the Brick Wally Loch. Tin boats were made from old biscuit tins and sailed in the foregoing lochs, or they could be pushed along the sands, imagining them to be their fathers' boats. Sandhoppers (sand lice) were scratched from the sand and killed and used as your fish catch. The Cat Loch was so named as this was where the surplus cats were drowned. There were no vets to destroy them and also no money to employ a vet. Most of the cats drowned were kittlins (kittens). They were placed in a hessian bag with a stone.

There were always arguments among the fishermen's children about which boat had the best engine, which could go fastest and which caught the biggest catch. Most of the young boys went on trips on their father's boats, especially on a Friday, as there was no danger of the boat lying out. Lying out meant that, if the drifter hadn't caught any herring, it wasn't worth the extra expense coming into port so the crew would search for a more likely herring spot. All boats returned to port on a Saturday as there was no Sunday work at this time. At the Yarmouth-Lowestoft fishing, some of the English boats went out on the Sunday but the Scots waited until after twelve o'clock.

Some of us used to go over the links on an outing with some hessian and poles to make a tent and also the necessary equipment and food to make a meal. There we would make chips, boil whelks or fry flukies, but more often than not we ended up with tummy trouble.

Fireworks were used mostly at New Year time. 'Guy Fawkes' didn't play much part in our way of life, only in our history lesson when 1605 meant the gunpowder plot. As mentioned earlier, we bought our squibs at Banker's Isie's, priced at ½d., 1d. and 2d. Sparklers and Chinese matches you could buy elsewhere. My father's shop didn't stock fireworks as we stocked paints, oils, paraffin and later petrol, so there was a fire risk and no fire engines available. A home-made device was to put a broken-up Chinese match in an old key with a nail in the hole and, by banging the key against a wall, causing an explosion.

The canal was yet another favourite haunt and here we collected poddicks' eggs (frog-spawn), tadpoles and bandies (sticklebacks). We also played about with frogs, eels could also be caught. The canal water was very warm to wade in although inclined to have a muddy bottom. The canal was formed when a Mr. Seller tried to drain the Loch of Strathbeg, but he gave up the idea due to the expense and the invading sand. This was towards the end of the eighteenth century.

Fummers were made by notching a thin piece of wood, attaching a string and whirling one round your head, when it produced a humming noise. Parachutes were made from a hanky and a piece of string. Furlers were carved from a piece of wood with a hole bored in the centre and this was attached to a handle and the furler could be coloured. The furler resembled a propellor. Hurlies, cairties, were made from the old pram wheels and boxes were used to race down the local hills. Mouth organs were much in evidence after the south fishing – gifts from parents.

Another simple device was putting a thin piece of string through the holes of a large button, winding it around and pulling it backwards and forwards. Sometimes a lucky bag would produce a serrated piece of tin which could be used in a similar manner, thus producing a whirring sound. You can see from the foregoing that we got amusement from some very simple devices. Towards the end of September when the bents were dry we would set them alight. This caused a huge blaze which spread for yards, driving out the vermin which we killed with sticks or stones; the dogs helped as well.

Girls' games

The lassies, at this time, played shoppies, hoosies and various other games, in which the boys sometimes joined. The names of the lassies around my age group were Betsy Strachan, Mugsee's Maggie, Putler's Bella, Putler's Meanie, Coxen's Jenny, Jessie Bella, Gena, Beena and Jeanie Don, Catherine and Mary Cranna, etc., etc.

Holding a buttercup under your chin to see if you liked butter, making daisy chains, blowing the head off a full-blown dandelion to tell the time, picking the petals off a daisy to prove love (she loves me, she loves me not). Peevers or boxies was another popular girls' game, where they pushed along a flat stone onto squares on the ground hopping on one leg. When skipping they had several songs which they chanted out, such as blacksugar, whitesugar, strawberry jam, tell me the name of your nice young man. They then went through the alphabet speeding up the rope (this speeding was known as a sattie) until the jumper tripped on a certain letter; say it was G, they would sing George and this continued to get a surname. It then continued with what kind of ring – gold, silver, etc. – what kind of dress – what kind of house, etc., etc.

Another game was throwing a ball against a wall, catching it after carrying out various manoeuvres like clapping hands and turning round without letting the ball touch the ground. The old favourite of stotting the ball on the ground and throwing a leg over it and singing the old ditty: one, two, three a-learie; four, five, six a-learie, and so on.

There were various ways of picking the mannie for a game:

The old one of eatel, oatel, black bottle, eatel, oatel, out;

Eennie, Meenie, Minnie Mo – OUT; and still another was:

'As I climbed up a Chinese stair I saw a lot of colours, some were blue and some were pink and some were the colour that you like best. Which colour do you like best?' A colour was then chosen, say green – the counter would then say G-R-E-E-N spells GREEN and O-U-T spells OUT.

One Potato, Two Potato, Three Potato, etc.

To play shoppies they would use sea sand for sugar, plaiks or lames (broken pottery) for money. For scales a straightened piece of metal hoop balanced on a stone or tin. The scale pans also used tins, perhaps old shoe polish tins which could be picked up on the sea shore. Milk would be produced by rubbing pottery against the rocks in a small rock pool, so colouring the water. Shells and coloured pebbles provided stores. Other odds and ends would be picked up from the beach, such as fish bones, seaweed and various articles which had been discarded.

Entertainments
Entertainments provided for the children were Sunday School Picnics, soirées, mission meetings, magic lantern shows. The picnic was invariably held in a field near Crimongate House. Originally the children and their parents were conveyed to the park in carts from nearby farms and later 'Wivers' bus. The picnics had the usual swings, races, sack race, three-legged race, barrow race, egg and spoon race, tug o'war, Aunt Sally, eating hanging biscuits; buns and tea were provided, the tea being served from shining brass kettles. The weather always seemed to shine on that day. After a pleasant day we were all conveyed back to the village by 'Wivers' bus. The Sunday School was held in the day school but different teachers were employed. One day one of the Sunday School teachers was speaking to her pupils about heaven and, turning to Sandy, said, 'What would you like to do when you get to heaven, Sandy?' Sandy, without blinking an eyelid, answered immediately, 'Lie among a strae (straw) and drink cream.'

At another children's meeting, the bairns were asked to bring something to represent a biblical text. One girl brought an old battered doll and her text was, 'These are they that have come through great trials and tribulations.'

The school soirée was held in the Kirky and was usually packed, the children all being dressed up in their braws. The parents were as nervous as the bairns in case their offspring failed in their party pieces.

The Mission Hall (The Bethel) was originally held in the converted garage of the Post Office, but later a new Bethel was built in Church Street near the butcher's premises. The meetings were very well attended and the collections were sent to help various charities, like new hospital beds, Quarriers' Homes, gifts to sick children in hospital, to name but a few.

The Mission Hall was taken over by the Salvation Army but was destroyed by fire and now a house has been built on this site.

The temperance walk was an event for the children as well as the adults. More will be said on this later.

Weddings were an attraction for the children as gleanings of sweets and other goodies were available, plus the collecting of money thrown by the bridal party and the throwing of rice by onlookers.

Hogmanay was another day of going around the doors singing the old favourite.

Rise up, guid wife, and shake yer feathers
Dinna think that we're beggars
We're bairnies come out to play
Rise up and gies oor hogmanay.

Making rhymes of words seen in windows or books was a pastime as well
– examples are:

PREFACE	Peter Rennie eats fish, Alex catches eels and reversed Eels catches Alex father eating raw peels
CONTENTS	Cows ought not to eat neeps to supper
EDINBURGH	E. Davie I never bade U rug grannie's hair
LETTERS	Lammy eating tirly tots eating raw sowens.

During the summer months the children ran about often barfit (bare-footed) or with sandals, a pair of shorts, and finished the summer as brown as berries. Your feet became hardened so that you could run over the rough rocks barfit without coming to any harm. The weather seemed to be much better then and, with a pair of briefs costing sixpence, you spent as much time in the sea as you did elsewhere. The pot and little potty near the village.

The golf course at this time had been forsaken, but we in St. Combs made a few holes between the rudder and the Cample and we used to smash the ball along with our brassies, baffies and mashies with a gutty and later an elastic golf ball.

I even managed to come to grief here having my head opened with a golf club swing by my opponent Alicky Toe, who was in greater distress than I was. A golf ball cost 6d. and clubs were usually hand-me-downs. Tees were unheard of, we used heaps of sand or fish bones.

With the introduction of the elastic ball, when the ball had seen better days we used to break it up and use the elastic for shooting paper pellets. In some golf balls there was an elastic bag filled with a putty paint substance. When repainting golf balls we put some white paint on our hands and rubbed and turned the ball in our hands.

My mother used to tease my cousin Cha (Charles West Junior) about the time the day school concert was performing Cock Robin. Cha was Cock Robin and fell asleep on the stage. At the picnics and soirées the children were handed a baggie with buns and apple. The Soirées were sometimes pretty rough occasions as, often even before the concert started, sweets and even fruit would be thrown about. My mother had an eye damaged at a concert which resulted in a detached retina. She had to lie in bed on her back for some time with a bandage over her eye, but it made no difference. Her eyesight was never very good and this accident made it worse. The hall was lit with paraffin lamps at this time and yet there were no fires in the Kirky.

An Ill Trickit Lot

Outside the school we often were an ill trickit lot
We termented mony o'ye but mostly those that chased
We climbed upon the hooses and chappit on yer doors
We dirled on yer windaes, threw steenies at yer cats
Sent phoney parcels tae ye, and thocht that it was fun.
Played fitba til the gloamin wi aboot twenty tae a side
Or maybe we played kniffie, or drooned moosie fae their holes
Wi bools and girds and furlers, we ran a ower the countryside
And in the better months, we fished the rocks and shories
We sometimes played wi quinies and broke their hoosies doon
We skippet played their boxies, but it wisna richt for loons.
We climbed the trees for craws eggs and pelted a aroon
My gracious me, we were an ill trickit lot.
There were a hantle mair things that were develment and fun
But if a mannie caught ye, a hiding you would get
A skelp across the chappers or a boot right in yer bum
And didna we deserve it – we were an ill-trickit lot.

Childhood Days

As I gid owr the Sanny Banks
On a bonny simmer's day
My barfit feet gid tae the queets
In the poodery shimmering sand
They were aa there, the hale ginge bang
Stripping aff their claes in haste
Tae dook inside the bar
The sea was calm and fine and haet
The quines were there as weel
And as we splashed and jumped aboot
Man, it was grand tae be a loon.

That wisna the day or yet the streen
But many years ago
A huntle waters gyen doon the burn
Since we splashed aboot the pot
A lot of those bairnies, have come and gone
To places far and wide
And some hae gaen tae places where
They'll hae eternal rest.
At that time we didna think
Of getting old and tottery
But only of the day that we
Would leave our beuks and skalie.

The children used to attend all the religious and political meetings in
the kirky and, as you got a little older, you could pick out the different
persuasions. At some of the religious services some of the audience used
to take a dwaam and be revived with smelling salts.

There were several religious revivals. There was one in the mid-nine-
teenth century around 1850 led by a Mr. Turner from Peterhead. I
remember Jack Troup, but he came much later. There was also a Pastor
Clark and his companion, Mr. Bell. They stayed with Charlie Ludo and
Mary. I don't think the St. Combs folk were very happy with these two.
This would have been in the 1920s.

The Village Hall

It may be caaed the village hall
In maest ither placies roon aboot
But tae us New Toon folkies
Oor hallie his aye been caaed 'The Kirky'
Since the time it wis biggit.
It's been eesed for mony different things
And bae folk fae a ower the wardle
Revivalists like Jock Troup or Turner
That made ye shak in yer seat
And mak some wifies tak a dwaan
Tae be kerrit oot for air
Or maybe it wid be Paulie Cruickshank
That sang and made ye lach
Till ye wis fit tae split

Or the aal-farrant temperance walk
Far ye hid tae sign the pledge
Afore ye quid tak pairt
Then there wis the walk soirée
That wi aye packit tae the gunnles
Wi a the folkies in their braws
Sooking sweeties for their hoasts
Handel's Messiah wis often sung
Wi zeal and dedication
They sometimes sang 'The Shepherd Boy'
Faur each did sing their chosen pairt.
Magsie she aye sang Abigail
And she made the Kirky ring
Ither roles were aye weel sung
By Cly, John Gick, and Jimky.
I canna name a' them that sung
If nae a soloist pairt they hid
A singer wid be in the choir
It wis a richt hamely nicht
That abody did enjoy
The hecklan meetings were held there
Wi names like Martin and Bob Boothby
And sometimes they got affa heated
Aboot the herber or the dole
The paraffin lamps they were a scutter
And a fire risk as weel
For a the things that were flung aboot
Gweed kens fou there wisna fire.
The Kirky it his seen the changes
And noo its jist anither wardle
New names, new folk, new times
But fou mony o' them speak 'The Doric'.

Transport

Before the coming of the train to the villages in 1903, they were pretty isolated. There were no lorries or cars; horse and cart were the only transport available for shifting heavy goods. For personal transport cabs would be used on special occasions, but for most folk it was 'Shanks's pony' that got you from A to B, say to Lonmay or Fraserburgh. Shanks's Pony meant that strong boots were required for the amount of walking that had to be done. The shoemaker at this time was in a small house not far from Forest's the joiners and Forsyth the blacksmith. The boots made to measure were really clumsy robust affairs, well equipped with 'tackets' (studs), and were known locally as 'Beetle Durks' so that for some time afterwards any tackety beets were known as beetle durks. Very few people would now know about these.

The carrying of gear to the yawls at the various shores was mostly done by the woman with creels. The women worked as hard as the men in the various duties and in the launching and landing of the yawls. Often when the men arrived home from the yawl fishing they would flop into a fireside chair and their wives would pull off all their fishing gear, boots, stockings, trousers, drawers – the lot – and some even shaved them and washed their faces.

The train was a real boon to the village as nets and other fishing gear could be transported to Fraserburgh. A story I remember about the opening of the Fraserburgh/St. Combs railway was about this lassie who saw the trainie coming out of the Cairnbulg station and was astonished to see this contraption moving along. The girl ran to her mother in great excitement shouting, 'Rin, midder, rin, the smiddy's awa and the streetie o hoosies ahint.' Translated, this would read – 'Run, mother, run, the blacksmith's shop has taken off with the street of houses behind it.' Not quite the same now, is it!

Locals were always getting their legs pulled about the trainie and once this smart lad addressed Jecky, saying, 'Jecky, that's a terrible train you have, it doesn't run on time.' Jecky replied, 'Fine div I ken that, it rins on coal, water and train lines.'

Yet another story is one about a visitor who got on the Aberdeen/ Fraserburgh train with Andra, who had had a little too much to drink. Andra had fallen asleep but awoke on coming towards Fraserburgh. On arriving in Fraserburgh he advised the visitor that the train did not go any further. The visitor said, 'You mean to say, this is a terminus.' Andra replied, 'Ae, that's richt.' The visitor then said, 'And is there a Mayor or Provost here?' 'Ae,' said Andra. The visitor then asked, 'And does he wear his chains of office?' 'Na, na,' Andra said, 'we dinna bother wi chines, we just let him rin lowse.'

The Aberdeen/Fraserburgh portion of the railway was completed in 1865, but due to various objections and snags, the Fraserburgh/St. Combs portion was not completed until 1903. The journey from Fraserburgh to St. Combs took twenty minutes for the five-mile run, with a stop at Cairnbulg station. There was a halt at Kirton, which was handy for the Fraserburgh Golf Course, and also a halt at Philorth (near Cairnbulg Castle). If the train had to halt at Philorth, it had a struggle to get up Mains Brae, especially in adverse weather conditions. There were several trains a day and these were usually timed to cater for the workmen, schoolchildren and fishwives. Some of the St. Combs office staff would come home for their lunch, and they used to jump off before the train had stopped, rush to their homes where the meal would be on the table, bolt their meal down and rush back to the station. The train stayed twenty minutes at St. Combs. The station staff would usually hold the train a few minutes if they saw anyone coming. The Cairnbulg people had more time for their meal. Tom Buchan (station Tom) with his doggie Rex were at the station for a number of years and Andrew Cheyne was the track surfaceman on track maintenance. He had been employed on the construction of the track itself. He was also School Janitor and, along with his wife, school cleaner. He was the father of Andy Cheyne the footballer, who signed for Glasgow Rangers.

The return fare was ten pence in the twenties, but regulars had a season ticket which worked out much cheaper and you could make as many daily journeys as you wished. The twenty-minute journey was handy for the children and their homework and impositions. If you did your homework on the train, it showed in the jerky writing and this resulted in an imposition of – 'I must not do my homework on the train.' The children used to frolic about in the carriage and on one journey we succeeded in pulling the communications cord, thus bringing the train to a halt. We got a real ticking off from the train staff. The train also carried freight, papers and mail, farm and fishing gear and goods. There was a special loading bank for heavy goods and also special trains for cattle. The butcher would go to the cattle marts in Aberdeen or Maud and buy a large consignment of beasts. These were driven to a large field near the station which we called 'King's Perk' (King's Jeck was the butcher).

Some of the young lands used to assist in cattle droves and we then got a hiding from the school teacher. The trainie proved to be a great boon for the fishwives, who boarded the trains at St. Combs and Cairnbulg and were then able to join the Aberdeen train and drop off at their particular station, such as Strichen, Maud, Auchnagatt, Brucklay, etc. They visited their particular houses with a creel and a basket. They would walk miles on their trips selling their fish or exchanging them for cheese, butter, fruit, eggs, etc., and they would then return to their station in the evening to catch the train home again. Fish vans and the closing of the railway put paid to the fishwives. Some of the fishwives were: Polly, Polly's Isie Ann, Betty Waker, Nellsie's Annie, Minnie, Peggy, Gena, Eppie and many others.

This story was told to me by my Uncle David (Pret) about Minnie, who was his aunt. David had been delegated to go with Minnie this particular day on her fish round. Minnie was a character and one of her attributes was that she was not backward in coming forward. Minnie and David were seated on the Aberdeen train when a young lady joined them, and Minnie, by her usual prodding, discovered she was a teacher. David intended to be a chemist and had just started his Latin classes. Auntie Minnie turned to David saying, 'Davie, you can speak Latin, hae a newsy wi the lassie in Latin and mak her feel at hame.' David told me his face must have been as red as a beetroot, and he was never so ashamed in his life and hoped the carriage floor would open up, but the lassie was in the same boat. In spite of all the baits and hidings, Davie would never go on a fish round with Auntie Minnie again.

A late train was run from Fraserburgh to St. Combs on the Saturday night, It brought the *Evening Express Green Final* and was known as the 'Boozer', and arrived at about ten o'clock. The young lads used to come to the station to see the carrying on of those who had got tipsy. I delivered the *Green Finals* through the village at a penny each; there was of course, no delivery charge then.

The train was also very useful for the fishworkers when they went to the South fishing at Yarmouth or Lowestoft, transporting their kists (trunks) and other equipment; often a special train would be provided to carry all the workers and their kists to the South ports. The fishermen used to send their dirty clothes home to their wives for washing; these were sent in baggies (coloured pillow cases) which as well as the clothes might have contained sweets, nuts or fruit for the children. The baggies were usually dispatched at the weekends and special mail bags would arrive at the villages on Monday or Tuesday. There were usually several bags and the Fraserburgh office would advise us as to how many there would be and we would go up to the station with either a barrow or our pony and float and, later still, our car. All this for the princely sum of 2s. 6d. per week. The children used to come to the office asking for their 'fadders baggie'. There were no Sunday collections or deliveries, but there was a collection on a Saturday. The station was both a place of joy and sadness. Many said their last farewells and some reunions took place there as well. Many of the people left for such places as America, Africa, New Zealand, India, and Australia, some never to return.

The evening mail was handed out from the office and there were usually several people waiting to ask for their mail. The various stamps told the story of the spread of the villagers to foreign parts. I have noted a few below.

Buchan	(Kirsten Cook)	–	New Zealand
Buchan	(Leeby Cook)	–	New Zealand
Buchan	(Pet's Peter's Andy)	–	America
Buchan	(Rogue)	–	Australia
Buchan	(Rogue's wife)	–	Australia
West	(Pret)	–	South Africa
Bruce	(Patsy Peter)	–	America
Buchan	(Sailor's Kirsten)	–	America
Buchan	(Anicky's George)	–	America
Buchan	(Gicks Alex)	–	America
Bruce	(Cattas Joe)	–	America
Buchan	(Mgt. Perky)	–	America
Buchan	(Toll)	–	America
Cow	(Duth)	–	America
Strachan	(Tandicks)	–	America
Buchan	(Plumber)	–	America
Bruce	(Den O'Howie)	–	America
Buchan	(Coxin's Chrissie)	–	America
Duthie	(Gran)	–	America
Baird	(Nellie)	–	South Africa
Buchan	(Go Fastie)	–	America

Many departed between the two wars during the depression and the failure of the fishing. Before cars and lorries became more commonly used, the train was used a lot by commercial travellers to the villages. Some of them used to send large crates with their samples and the traveller would arrive to show his wares and take his order. One I remember was Ogilvie's (hardware, etc.) of Shoe Lane, (Mr. Martin) Aberdeen; another was a Mr. Donaldson of Glasgow and he used to spend his holidays with us at the Post Office. The travellers then were a very gentlemanly lot and were friends; in fact, my brother was named after three travellers – Sylvester, Davidson, Fairweather – which is rather a mouthful. In 1965 Dr. Beecham finished off the trainie and its departure was, to the villagers, like losing a friend. Cairnbulg and Inverallochy had a bus service (Joe's Bus) before the train stopped, but St. Combs got a bus service when the train stopped. On the last day of the trainie many villagers turned up to get a last run and to say a last farewell, some perhaps with a tear in their eye.

With the closure of the Aberdeen/Fraserburgh/Peterhead sections of the Buchan line, the tracks have been uplifted and the village stations have disappeared and, at St. Combs, housing has encroached on the station's precincts. The end of an era, thanks to Beecham.

Even before the train service packed up, more and more goods were being sent by road, as it meant a door-to-door service and less handling and was much cheaper. Local carters were 'Cairter Alex', Sandy Wiver and several from Peterhead and Fraserburgh such as French, Reid, Eadie and Sutherlands. Cairter Alex ran an old Model T Ford Lorry. He used to carry a watch which was always fast, so that on a journey from St. Combs to Fraserburgh, on looking at the town clock in the Broch, you discovered that you had travelled at about a mile a minute, whereas if you had been in a hurry, you would have got out and walked. Alex always wore a cap to cover his bald head. He maintained that his hair had been blown out by the speed of his lorry. The following story relates to one of the fishwives whose son was getting married. The women usually looked after the purse strings, and usually arranged all the preliminaries as well as the wedding itself. The lad wishing to find out his financial position addressed his mother as follows: 'Midder, faur div I ston?' His mother replied, 'Ston, sinny, ye ston on yer ain twa feet and if it wisna for my quintry creel, ye widna be stonen the wye that ye ston.' This would translate:
Son – 'Mother, what is my financial position?'
Mother – 'Your financial position is all due to my hard work selling fish around the countryside.'

One of the first cars.

Us young lads didn't like the fishwives coming into our carriage as they stifled our activities, so we used to crowd round the windows giving the impression that our carriage was full. They would have stopped us playing cards, doing our homework or just generally larking about.

Transport

In days lang seen, twas Hobson's choice
And that was Shanks's Pony
The creel it was the fishers' friend
Tae shores and countryside
In Nineteen three the trainee came
And wasn't it a blessing
It opened up the great outside
And lengthened the horizons
The Broch before was miles awa
But noo was only meenits
And Aberdeen the great unseen
Wis jist a pleasant journey

The lorries came and motor cars
The village got its streeties
And progress still – The Beecham way
He stopped the trainie rinnen
A bus now runs for all to use
But mony have their carries
And some day soon there may be
A helicopter service.

The Post Office and Shop

My mother was the village Postmistress before her marriage. The Post Office was originally at 4 High Street (George Breecy's) and then shifted to 7½ Mid Street (Polly's Half House). My father took over the shop from his father (Pet's Peter). Pet's Peter built the house Seaview and retired there, his daughter Maggie married Jimky and stayed in Seaview. My father's shop was just across the road from the Post Office and, when he married my mother in 1908, the Post Office was integrated with the shop. My mother kept the title of Postmistress but played little part in the running until after my father's death. Shortly after my father took over the Post Office, a rather pompous Head Postmaster from Fraserburgh came out and criticised the office set-up. My father was rather busy at the time and was annoyed with the manny and told him to take his Post Office elsewhere as he didn't particularly want it, as it was more bother than it was worth, paying only a pittance or a wage and sitting there rent free. The manny with his assistant spent a fruitless day in the village, but couldn't find any takers and had to return cap in hand and plead with my father to keep it on. This he did, and never had any further trouble from this 'manny'. The Fraserburgh Head Postmasters changed quite a bit over the years. Many became close friends of ours and my parents used to visit them at the new offices or retirement homes

The payments for the office work of the Post Office was 10s. 0d. (50p.) per week, 2s. 6d. for phone attendance and 2s. 6d. for mail attendance. These amounts continued for many years. When I used to deliver telegrams, it was 1½d. for a village delivery and 3d. a mile outwith the village. A long distance telegram could earn 1s. 3d. and the cost of sending a telegram was 1d. a word or 9d. for twelve words. The *Evening Mail* was collected from the four o'clock train and handed out from the

Post Office, St. Combs.

office. Any left over were delivered by the morning Postman – John Strachan (Postie John) – who used to cycle from Inverallochy and deliver the morning mail. He was followed by Jimmy Lumsden, also from Inverallochy. Postie John's daughters, Maggie and Janet, ran the Inverallochy Post Office. Another daughter, Lizzie, worked in our shop before she married and went to America. Postie John was one of the old school, a real gentleman. He was a gentle obliging man, nothing ever troubled him. The deliveries were taken over by Fraserbugh postmen who came in postal vans. The names of some of these were: Sandy Simpson, Sandy White, Tom Whyte, John McKay, but to name a few. They were all supplied with their morning cuppa by my mother. Even from an early age I helped with the telegrams and postal deliveries, especially during the South fishing season.

Many of the older folk were unable to read or write and signed their pensions with an X. Some of the letters had been pre-written and a space left to fill in the week's cran catch. I remember once delivering mail to a house and being met in the doorway by a frothing stream of liquid. The wifie came running out exclaiming, 'Thank goodness you have come, Davie, I put the pudding in the pot and she won't stay in.' I went to investigate to discover she had put a new type of washing powder in the milk instead of pudding mixture.

We were also asked to fill up pension forms and other documents. We also had to witness the X some used when signing their pensions. I remember one gentleman handing in his form and asking for it to be checked by us and, where it asked for type of property, he had written 'Nae hoose noo'. Another pensioner, on receiving his first pension, was asked what it was like to be a pensioner and he replied, 'Man, he's a fine chielly, the government – it's the day the coo calfs.'

Up until the thirties, the Post Office had the only telephone in the village and it was on a party line basis. St. Combs received five rings, Inverallochy Post Office four rings, Cairnbulg coastguards three rings, Fraserburgh coastguards two rings and Rattray coastguards six rings. These were split up into separate lines at a later date and later still became automatic when the rural automatic telephone exchanges were introduced at Inverallochy, Lonmay and St. Fergus. It was sometimes very difficult to get the older folk to speak on the telephone. They seemed to be afraid of it. My granny wouldn't have spoken on it for love or money. I can recall one woman coming to the telephone to speak to her son and she broke down because she could hear him but was unable to see him. An other time, I delivered a telegram to a woman, who, on opening it, remarked, 'I

would ken oor Geordie's writing anywhere.' Little did she know that it
had been dictated from the telegraph room in Fraserburgh.

There were many girls in the shop from my toddling days to when I left
home: Kirsten Bide (Christian Buchan), Mary Buchan (Fraserburgh),
Lizzie Strachan (Inverallochy Post Office), her sister Janet Strachan,
daughters of Postie John; the other daughter Maggie, and mother, tended
the Inverallochy Office; Mabel Greig and her niece, Irene Greig. Most left
to get married or take up other duties. I helped out in the shop and other
duties, like car driving, painting, etc., but I was never very keen or very
good, although it could be very amusing at times. As I have already
mentioned, the Buchans' and the Bruces' predominance could become
very confusing if the proper names and addresses were not given on the
letters, etc. The following is a list of names of people living in East Street
and Church, which illustrates this point:-

East Street	East Street
No. 1 Buchan (Putler's Sam)	No. 12 Buchan (Fleppy)
No. 2 Buchan (Hope)	No. 13 Buchan (Daisy)
No. 3 Cow (Adie's Cow)	No. 14 Bruce (Billicky)
No. 4 Buchan (Mannie)	No. 15 Cow (Petrie Nip)
No. 5 Buchan (Spottie)	No. 16 Buchan (Bob & Betty)
No. 6 Buchan (Buckie)	No. 17 Strachan (Non)
No. 7 Buchan (Annicky's Robbie	No. 18 Buchan (Magity)
No. 8 Buchan (Eppie)	No. 19 Strachan (Lizzie Watt)
No. 9 Buchan (Putler)	No. 20 Buchan (Tonner)
No. 10 Buchan (Officer)	No. 21 Buchan (Dodicky)
No. 11 Buchan (Patty)	No. 22 Jack (married a Buchan)

Some of these names changed over the years but most remained as
Buchans until very recently.

Church Street	Church Street
No. 1 Buchan (Dood)	No. 4 Buchan (Butcher)
No. 2 Buchan (Boxy)	No. 5 Buchan (Cookie)
No. 3 Buchan (Gaggers)	No. 6 Buchan (Wullicky)

The Mission Hall (The Bethel) at the end of Church Street was run by a
Buchan, my father Patty, so you can imagine the Postman's nightmare in
finding the right Buchan if the letter was addressed to Buchan St. Combs
or Buchan East Street, and this sometimes happened. There was a good

crab trade with South Markets and the letters were often poorly addressed but the office staff, knowing the crab fishermen, could usually spot the one concerned.

The office received many phone calls from Peterhead and Fraserburgh to get someone from the village to speak on the 'phone. This often took some time, especialy if the party was in Charleston or at the top of High Street. Quite often the caller expected you to fetch the person right away. The call for Fraserburgh was 2d. and the charge to Peterhead was 5d. These were what were called 'call office fee' and each had to be recorded in a local register which was checked from the Fraserburgh exchange in the evening. I have alrady mentioned that telegrams, as often as not the long distance telegrams, arrived on a Saturday night which meant a long journey, sometimes having to push your bike up some of the farm roads which were not properly surfaced. Typical of this was Links Cottage where the Gamekeeper lived. This was near the Loch of Strathberg and a typical telegram might read, 'Shooting Party arriving early Monday, please make necessary arrangements' or, 'Two tons of potatoes Monday morning'. I used to take the bicycle, originally with oil lamps, and the dogs (Tibby and Jock) on many of the trips and they did enjoy it. Tibby was a wire-haired fox terrier – a real 'ratter' – whilst Jock was a curly-haired black retriever. We had several dogs during my years at home, but Jock and Tibby were my favourites.

The Local Butchers had no 'phone until the thirties and we got many calls for them. Their shop was just a hundred odd yards from ours and in sight, so we had a whistle which we used to bring them to the 'phone. If they were busy in the slaughterhouse, we used to run down the nearby lane and fetch them. A large roast was handed over at New Year Time for our services. We got many night disturbances, especially for doctors, there being no resident doctor in the village. The doctors had to come from Crimond, 'Dr. Reid', or we had to get some of the Fraserburgh doctors. These were Doctors Trail, Webster, Beedy and McConnachie.

Very often, our stores were left unlocked, but the dogs always gave us warning if anyone was about. The carriers would carry goods into the store but the dogs wouldn't allow them to take anything out. To illustrate this better, our neighbour 'Leeby Anne' was helping my mother to clean and she had gone into the store to get some whitening. She put the bowl in the barrel to get it, but as she was coming away, Jock took hold of her arm but didn't bite. He only let go when my father appeared to answer Leeby Anne's shouts. Her arm was unmarked.

Some of the visitors used to describe the shop as the 'Harrods' of the North and you could get anything from an anchor to a needle. No doubt an overstatement, but there certainly was a good selection of food and clothing and household articles. Some of the old folk had some strange names for certain articles and it took some time for new assistants to get the know-how. Some of the names originated from the Franco-Scottish alliance or even the 'Strandloupers', who were the supposed original inhabitants. Loaf Bread was: French loaf, sole loaf, cottage loaf, pan loaf and so on. Bun names were uphills, sair heedies, muck middens, flee cemetries, currant douce, fairens, rice, fardens, and smachries were fancy biscuits, etc., etc. Tinned fruit was for special occasions like the walk and perhaps a Sunday. One customer used to ask for a tin of yon things like the reeds o' eggs (apricots). There were certain customers who were very awkward, i.e. one woman asked for a two-cup teapot, which I produced and was going to wrap it up when she said, 'Na, na, laddie., I want to see it pooring', so I had to fill it up with water and demonstrate. The teapot cost about 9d. Toffee bars were in the ½d. to 1d. range. Most sweets were 2d. to 4d. a quarter. Chocolate bars ½d., 1d. and 2d. Lucky tatties were a favourite and this was a lump of hard candy coated with cinnamon and sometimes a ½d. (bawbee) wrapped in paper was concealed in the candy. Other sweets were called blacksugar straps, striped balls, soor plooms (sour plum), sweet tobacco, sugar mice, sweety bools (ogo pogo eyes) – these were large circular balls which you hardly were able to get into your mouth and, as you sucked them, they changed colour. Another item was black sugar, a hard liquorice stick about six inches long costing 3d. The children, especially the girls, used to buy a ½d. or 1p. worth, flake off small chips and put them into a bottle with water and shake until they were melted. They then added further small pieces until the mixture was jet black. This was called black sugar water and had a laxative effect. Other items sold were caps, 2s. 6d., shirts 5s. 0d., suits for as little as 30s. 0d., bicycle equipment, wireless batteries, golf balls, daily and weekly newspapers, patent medicines such as aspirins, various salts, syrup of figs, asthma cures, liver and kidney pills, lysol, carbide, cartridges, bandages, boots, shoes (10s. 0d. and 15s. 0d.), knitting wool, blankets, sheets, towels, stockings, socks, razors, clocks, dyes, dried and fresh fruit, oatmeal, cheese butter, jam, sugar, spices, etc., etc.

Prices were cheap but the wages and pensions were low. The wages were round the £2 area, the pension was 10s. 0d., so that very few lived in Quality Street (1930). In the thirties the van trade increased and the local shop trade fell. Further diversification was necessary. Ice cream was a seasonal trade and some items were brought in at special times, like sandals for picnics, sensens for a soirée – these were aromatic liquorice pellets for soothing the singer's throat and giving the breath a pleasant smell, and they cost 2d.

My father stopped selling tobacco and cigarettes but after his death my mother added them to the shop shelf again. It could be said that the shop never closed for even before or after the shop closed, as we lived on the premises we were always available for handing out the odd item and to send telephone messages. There was a compulsory nine to ten duty rota on Sunday for telegrams.

The official lunch hour was twelve to one but, although the door was closed, we were still available for duty. The dogs used to recognise the rattle of the twelve to one closing sign and they set up their barking in anticipation of their walk and run on the beach and their splash in the sea. Even during your twelve to one break you always kept one ear open for the telephone and also the odd caller for a message.

During the early thirties, after I qualified as a wireless operator, I wired the premises for electricity and installed a 50 volt DC generating plant and it did valiant services until the Hydro Power arrived. The shop catered for school picnics for some of the country schools. There were one or two holiday campers who came regularly and often visited the shop. The beaches and bents are a paradise for children, with unrestricted freedom and safe sea bathing, especially when the sea is out. The Duncans of Tilly Corthie, of tin mine fame, used to come down from their country home and camp on the links near the Cample. They often visited the shop. Their relations are still around in Aberdeen.

During the 1939 war, evacuees from Glasgow were billeted in the village and most of them were out of their depths. My mother had two of the teachers staying with her. The evacuees were accustomed to eat from the chip shop fare and didn't take kindly to the St. Combs meals of soups, meats and puddings. Once, while I was home on leave and in the shop, this little lad came into the shop asking for a 'titany'. I kept asking the lad to say it more slowly but it was always 'titany'. Irene appeared and explained that the wee fella wanted a teet for his little sister Annie. Simple, isn't it?

Another story concerns one of our paper boys, who was a very consci- entious lad. Evening papers were 1d. at the time or 6d. a week, with no delivery charge. Charlie had been owing three weeks' papers. Charlie said

to the paper boy, 'Weel, boy, that will be achteen pence.' The paper boy
said, 'Na Charlie, 1s. 6d.'

Most of the houses were spotlessly clean and during the summer months
some of the families would live in outhouses or an annex and when you delivered a paper you daren't enter a house, you simply shouted 'Paper'. Some
houses were regularly painted, the stonework being in black and white.

My father had close ties with Charleston and Helenie, the midwife,
used to visit our home very often. Ton's Pat was another visitor and he
found his wife there, Maggie Taylor, who worked with us at the time and
her sister Betsy followed when she left. They came from Broadsea
Fraserburgh. Another association my father had with Charleston was that
his shop trading code was Charleston. This meant that when marking his
goods the word 'Charleston' represented the figures 1 to 10. To the
uninitiated, this meant that if the code on an article had the letter C/H on
it, the article would have cost 1s. 2d. with letters A/L 3/5. This became
important at the time of the sales or the clearing of stock.

The last Public House was in Charleston in No. 4, where Helenie lived,
followed by Ton's Pat and now by his daughter Margaret. No. 1 was occu-
pied by Baker Andy who worked with my father, No. 2 The Gicks; No. 3
Duncan Buchan Family; No. 4, Ton's Pat; No. 5 Buchan (Dags); No. 6
(Bucks); No. 7 Buchans; No. 8 More Gicks; No. 9 Another Gick; No. 10
Greevie; No. 11 Katie's Jeck; No. 12 Acky; No. 13 Hackett; No. 14 Andra
May; No. 15 Dohs Dody; No. 16 Duncans; No. 17 Dannels. There were
various changes over the years and these are bye names. Most of them are
Buchans.

We had a good supply of daily and weekly papers. The *Press and
Journal* was the most popular paper, followed by the *Daily Express, Daily
Record* and *Daily Herald*. There were one or two orders for others. The
Evening Express was the only evening delivery. During the holiday sea-
son the odd local paper would be especially ordered, like the *Dundee
Courier*, during the Dundee holidays, and the *Scotsman* and *Glasgow
Herald* during their fare week. The weekly papers *People's Journal,
Weekly News, Beano, Dandy, Christian Herald, Sunday Companion, Peo-
ple's Friend, Secrets, My Weekly, Welcome, British Weekly* and an odd
copy of the *Topical Times, Exchange & Mart, Fishing News, Tit Bits,
Weekly News of the World, Picture Post* and *John Bull*, etc., etc. Alas, a
few of these have now departed the scene. The one that was the greatest
loss was the *People's Journal*.

Another duty to be carried out was to send a report of any interesting
local news to the papers – the Aberdeen Papers and to the *People's*

Journal. It might be a report on a walk, a concert, a picnic, death insertions, but they never seemed to bother about marriage or birth insertions. There were no Sunday papers sold by any of the shops but some would perhaps be sold on the Monday. The unsold papers were useful to the chip shop when it opened or for eating your tatties and herring. The paper wholesaler for papers other than the *Journal* and *Evening Express* were Holmes and Company. All the papers came by train. There were no van deliveries until much later. The papers were in the 1d. to 2d. range. Dailies were 1d., apart from the *Press and Journal*, which was 1½d. Weeklies were 2d. and this stayed constant for years, not like today's inflationary prices. Postage stamps were ½d. for an unclosed letter (say an account), postcards 1d., ordinary letter 1½d. Parcels were in the 6d. to 1s. 6d. range. None of the shops opened on a Sunday.

The Shoppie

There was a little shoppie
And eence I called it hame
They came fae near and far
To buy what we did sell
And fit there wisna in it
It would be hard for me to name.
The Shoppie hid the Post Office
And did ither things as well.
They selt sugar, soap and biscuits
And tatties meal and jam
And for your constipation
They hid cascara, figs and salts
There wis putty, paint and varnish
Wi' stockins, socks and sheen
We hid apples cheese and butter
Ae and worsit, pots and pans
Bonnets, sarks and buttons
And papers, claith and speens
They'd even charge your batteries
Or tak ye tae be wed
Pensions stamps and licenses
Wi' nails or tacks or preens
There were cartridges and carbide
Skalie, Sklates and beans

Pens and beukes and pencils
Sweeties, saut and rice
Girdles pails and sodas
Elastic, lard and spice
Coffees, teas and treacle
Bibles, snuff and tobacco
Wi' toys or breed or fat.
We hid linners we hid drawers
We hid ointments, peels and potions
There were table cloths or jeelies
There were dyes there were watches
As well as paraffin and matches
Bricks or ties or hankies
Wi' bloomers, steys or beets
And if there was a picnic
We could supply the eats.
It was a mixer maxter lot
And that is just a sample.
Some they were upon the reef
And ithers on the fleer
Some were in gless cases
While ithers were in drawers
And some were up on shelvies
That needed steps to reach
And if we didn't have it
We'd order it for you
Such things as a wireless
Or a made to measure suit
A fancy lamp or bicycle
Or a special wadding gift
But a' that has gone now freens
The folkies have departed
The shoppie noo is shuttered up
A memory of the past.

The Fishing

The local herring fishing boats started their season with what was called the 'riggin oot'. This entailed the fisherman going into Fraserburgh and preparing the boat for the season. The boat would have been put on the slip or pontoon, her bottom scraped and painted and all other painting work and repairs carried out. The black squad (driver and fireman) would have cleaned out the boiler by chipping off the hardened deposit and cleaning it out. The fisherman would then have seen that all the leader rope, bowes and tows and nets were all in order and then they were 'redded' into the hold.

On the Saturday the women folk with their kids went into Fraserburgh to give the cabin and galley a good clean up, the 'caffseks' being refilled with fresh caff from the ferm. The beds were made. During this time the kids would have been romping aboot or catching podlies (small saithe). The women prepared a bun feast with fancy biscuits and tea sweetened with condensed milk. After having our fill it was up to Galloway's shoppie for candy and also some to take home to my Grannie. She would never have forgiven me if I had been to the riggin oot and not got her a box of Galloway's home-made candy (6d.). My aunty Maggie (Mugsie) usually took me to the *Ocean Searcher* riggin oot (FR.75). A penny worth of chips were also a must for all. We usually went in on the eleven o'clock train and came back on the four o'clock train. On the Monday the boats went off to the fishing grounds to search for the 'Silver Darlings'. There were no radars or sonars in those days, the tell-tale sign of the sea birds diving, the activities of the queetie, whales (Phals), looper dogs, etc., etc. The boats' cooks were usualy older men or young boys making their first trip.

This story was told to me by Tandyke's Sandicky, who was involved in this episode. On his first day at sea this young cook asked Sandy about

53

making boiled rice. He then asked how much he would put into the pot for the whole crew. Sandy replied to put in a jugful. The young lad misunderstood and took this to be a jugful of rice for each man instead of milk. Shortly afterwards the young man came running up to Sandy, asking for his help as the galley was being flooded with rice. Operation Clean Up was carried out, with the surplus rice being thrown overboard. Perhaps this contributed to the good catch of herring they had the next day. The fishermen have my sympathy, for they had a hard life, some men suffering from sea sickness all their lives, especially on a Monday morning. I ventured forth in my Uncle Beedie's (Andra West) boat, the M. A. West (FR.240). What with the smell of the herring and the heat in the galley I spent a miserable time and after coming ashore I was still rocking about. I also recall John McKenzie, a deckhand, coming up to me in the wheel house saying, 'Are you sick, Davey? Eat this and you'll feel better.' He produced a great big door step (thick) of two slices of bread with the syrup running out of the sides. 'It will put a lining on your stomach, Davey.' I don't think I had any stomach left to line for most of it had gone over the side. We had a good catch that day, no doubt due to my sea sickness.

Beedie was a very successful fisherman. He was also known as 'Full Butt' (full steam ahead) for after hauling the nets, his instructions to the black squad were, 'Come noo, Tonner, a ye can gie her full butt.' The earlier you were in port the more likely you were to get a better price for your catch. Beedie used to go all over the place to fish – Fraserburgh, Lerwick, Stronsay, Stornaway, Mallaig, Ireland, Lowestoft, Holland, Shields, etc. He also went white fish fishing with his drifter and a smaller boat a 'baldie'. They used smaalin (small lines), fishing for haddock, etc. He used the small auxiliary boat, named *The Quest*, to augment the drifter by using the shallower water. A cook with my uncle told me the story about another cook during the 1914 war. The cook, who was working on a naval drifter, had heard that there was to be an inspection of the drifters by an Admiral. Andra, the cook, was busy lifting the duff (fruit pudding) out of the pot when a uniformed officer appeared at the galley. Andra, thinking it was the Admiral, got rather flustered and addressed the gentleman thus: 'Sir, are you the Admiral? We'll hud (hold) this duff 'till I salute ye.' The Admiral turned out to be a fisherman's representative.

There is another story about Andra, who was a real character. This time he was a cook in a drifter at the South fishing. One weekend he and his chum went ashore to get a bonnet for Andra. Andra went into a shop and asked for a cap with the snoot (peak) at the side. Many of the fishermen were wearing their bonnets with the peak at the side. I suppose it was less likely to blow off in this position. The shop assistant was about round the bend, what with language and not knowing what was required and having been reduced to his last box of caps; Andra's chum, tired waiting, walked into the shop and sized up the situation. He turned the bonnet to the side and Andra was well pleased, paid up and walked away.

Large fleets of boats went South to Yarmouth or Lowestoft, often stopping at Shields or Grimsby on the way down. For those left behind it could be a very worrying time as there were often very bad storms at this time of the year. The departure of the fleets from the Peterhead and Fraserburgh areas drew a large number of support staff with them as curers, salesmen, office staff, gutters, packers, freshers, coal merchants and perhaps some children and wives. In the period between the war large shots (catches) of herring were being landed at the fishing ports and the large catches resulted in a big drop in prices. Prices fell to 2s. 6d. per cran (four baskets) and often when the gut factories couldn't cope with this influx, the herring would have to be dumped at sea by the fishermen or sometimes hired labour (what a waste). Catches of over 100 crans were very common at this time. This over-fishing no doubt led to the present day decline.

After all the toil and trouble over a fishing season the boats would often finish in debt. Some fishermen didn't pay a great deal of attention to the financial side, leaving it all to the salesmen. The actual salesmen in Fraserburgh at that time were Walkers (Adam Brown), Irvines (Peterkin), Bloomfields (Charlie Buchan, St. Combs) and there were some salesmen that came up from the South for the season (Hobsons). The salesmen used what were called 'runners'. The runners waited on the pier for their company boats to arrive and then these runners, with a member of the crew, took the herring sample to the sale ring where the catch was sold, either in total to one buyer, or split up between two or more buyers, the buyers being curers, canning factories, freshers or the gut factory, etc. Runners also delivered the boat's mail from the various salesmen's offices.

Before the boats left the South fishings, the crew used to visit the shops for presents for their wives and chilren. The skipper of a boat had said that he had got a pair of 'steys' (corsets) for his wife. Some of the rest of the crew also purchased steys in fancy boxes. As the boat was approaching the Broch Harbour, the Skipper was seen to throw the box overboard. The crew assumed that the Skipper had chickened out and they weren't going to be the fall guys and classed as 'Jeannie Anns' (cissies) so they threw their boxes and the steys overboard, only to discover that the Skipper had taken his steys out of the box before throwing it overboard.

St. Combs drifters in use at this time were: *Northern Scot, Brothers Gem, Strathbeg, Pittendrum, Caupona, Girl Evelyn, M.A. West, Auchmedden, Ocean Searcher, Millburn, Gowanhill, Citreon, Light, Harvest Gleaner, Gloamin, Boy John, Star O'Buchan.* The boats when they got older could be purchased for a few hundred pounds and more often than not finished up on the local beaches as scrap. Several finished on the St. Combs shores to be broken up and sold as firewood by Putler & Sons at St. Combs (Buchans).

Some of the boats had rather fancy names and the runner (Onze) had great difficulty with these names, even the young runners had trouble pronouncing them: *Nulli Secundus, Spes Meleor, Poseidon, Cornucopia, Thermopylea, Archimedes,* etc. Onze was great on his diminutives, sticking on his i and es. For example, *The Jeannie Leaskie, Bounteous Seakie.* Onze was a kindly soul and greatly liked by the young lads. Catta was another runner for Walkers and came from St. Combs and was one of the 'Nicka' clan. He was always rushing about. He raced up and down with the herring samples. He was very good with his gun and shot on the links and on nearby farms during his leisure hours.

My Academy school chum, Jimmy Noble, worked for one of the English Firms (Hobsons). I worked for Walkers, my Uncle Beedie's agents. Our weekly wage was 10s. 0d. (50p.).

Others who welcomed the fishing season were the women. The same gutting crew often travelled around to the various ports, Lerwick, Yarmouth, Fraserburgh, etc. Most of the women crews stayed in what were called the huts, very spartan places they were but very jolly as well. They were called to duty by one of the fish curers' staff perhaps shouting 'Come on, lassies, get up and get your clouts on.' This referred to the cloths they wound round their fingers and heads to minimise the effects of the salt and gutting knife. A profit of £20 for the season would be pretty good – changed days now.

There is a story about a gutting crew who used to stay with a woman called Martha in Lerwick. She was a bit of a hypochondriac and was always ill. She said to the girls, 'Noo, lassies, when I die, I would like you to see that I am burned.' Cremations at this time was a rarity. 'Na, na,' said the lassies, 'yer nae dying, you're just like Martha in the Bible.' Martha had her way and the lassies promised to fulfil her wishes, but one of the girls said, 'Ye ken, Martha, the nearest crematorium is in Aberdeen and we would have to take you down in the North boat.' Martha replied, 'Weel, weel, lassies, in that case just forget it for I am aye sick on the North boat.'

The working hours for the gutters were long and hard and in a busy day could range from six in the morning until ten at night under the glare of the carbide lamps, the yards filled with chatter and singing. Freshers bought the early catches, packed them in different sized boxes with a scoop of ice and they were sent to the markets in special trains – Billingsgate Market, etc. The kippering firms were other buyers, also the canning factories such as McConnachie in Fraserburgh and Crosse & Blackwell in Peterhead. The big buyers were the curers such as Dunbars of Fraserburgh and Sinclair Buchan of Peterhead.

The gutting yard huts were a great attraction for the males, especially at the weekends, and at certain stations there was said to be very handy ladders lying around so that the huts could be reached surreptitiously. Many a fisherman found his wife via the fishing romances.

Lewis and Harris men joined the boats as hired men, several with the St. Combs boats.

The opening of the St. Combs railway drew some of the yawl fishers to the herring fishing. Another increase was due to the improvement in the type and size of boats. In earlier days an open-decked boat was used, but during a very bad storm there was great loss of life with this type of boat and therefore decked boats came into use with scaffies, fifies and later zulies. Towards the turn of the century, drifters and motor boats super-seded the sail boats. The original drifters were known as 'pipe stalkies' because they had very thin funnels. These early drifters could revert to sail if necessary and vice versa as requested. They didn't trust the engines. The boats were often spotted in a crowded harbour by their funnel colour and distinguishing marks.

This anecdote concerns a day tripper who had come off a bus and went up to this worthy at the harbour and asked if he could tell him where the urinal was. The worthy said, 'I couldn't say I've heard of her, but if you could tell me what kind of funnel she has, I might be able to spot her in the throng.'

The drifter was in its heyday just before and after the First World War. Many drifters were taken over by the Admiralty in both wars, being used for such purposes as mine sweeping and as tender vessels. One village skipper was known as V.C. Joe for his heroic 1914 deeds. St. Combs fishermen were on the *Daisy II* which was a tender to the *Royal Oak* when she was sunk by a German submarine. Also, Andrew Buchan (Daisy) was awarded the D.S.C. for his trips in a drifter to the Dunkirk beaches. I was on duty in a defence station in Orkney when the *Royal Oak* was sunk and there was quite a stir on that night. Scapa defences were tightened.

The local drifters and yawls were registered under the Fraserburgh letters FR, Peterhead was PD. One of the older fishermen told me how much they were indebted to my grandfather and father for the way they treated them as regards provisions and debt. He said they often kept them in food during the winter months until they could repay them during the better months when they were able to fish; some of them never were able to pay. Some of them had to borrow, to pay for a wedding and funeral expenses. A box of cod would be sold for 2s. 6d. at this time (12½p.). My father suffered a breakdown at this time caused by bad debt. He eventually burned the whole lot, cut out the herring net trade and kept a tighter grip on debt, but lost a few customers in the process.

Some of the yawl men were: James Buchan (Officer), Bruce (Onzie), Bruce (Johnny Breecie), W. Bruce (Nicka's Wulzie), A. Buchan (Sailor), Bruce (Quarrie), Buchan (Choppy), Strachan (Tandick), Buchan (Dody Fitie), Billy Organ, Muff, Fite, Kirky Dave, Daisy, Non, Nonter, Petrie Nip, etc., etc. The yawls had such names as: *Gemini, Viola, Zephyr, Peggy, Nellie, Quiet Waters, Myosotis*. The yawls operated from the various shores, depending on where the crew lived. The Kittyloch was usually used by the North Side fishermen from the Charleston and Bridge Street areas. The Cample was used by the South side yawls, the New Shore by the middle yawl men. Some landing points would become silted up by sand and were made unsuitable for landings, especially during bad weather.

The women played a large part in the yawl fishing activities; they carried the fishing gear in their creels from the houses to the shores, sometimes over a mile away. The women also assisted in the launching of the yawls, carrying the gear and the men to the boats. A similar process was again gone through when the yawls landed. They 'redded' and baited lines and assisted with the 'pairten' of the fish. The fish would be carried in their creels to the station for the Fraserburgh market, sold locally to the fishwives or kept for storage and the making of 'hairy tatties'. If the fish were to be kept by the crew they would be 'pairted' (apportioned). Say there were three in the yawl crew, three heaps of fish would be made (of equal size). One of the crew would turn his back and another would ask, pointing to one of the bundles of fish, 'Fa's is this?' (Whose fish are those?) and the person whose back was turned would answer, 'Yours, Wullie', then he would be asked a second time and would say 'Jeemsie's'; the last lot would be his own. This 'pairten' method was used by tradesmen (joiners, etc.) when they went on fishing trips after work.

The winter curing of fish consisted of splitting, gutting, scrubbing clean and steeping and heavy salting. The fish were then laid out on racks or dykes or other flat surfaces and turned regularly in the drying summer winds and sun. When they were bone hard they were stored in a dry place. My, if you got a wallop on the head with a dry fish it could knock you out. There was no harbour at St. Combs, although several attempts were made to raise funds, such as concerts, collections, and afterwards a rough stone dyke shelter was erected at the Kittyloch which was not very effective. Due to the lack of a harbour, the yawls had often great difficulty in making a landing if the weather was bad; this was due to the various sand bars at the shores. If the wind got up when the yawls were at sea, it could lead to large waves breaking on the bars. The boaties waited outside the breaking waves until there was a sma' (lull), then they rowed like mad to get over the bar before the waves got up again. This was a tricky operation. If the storm was particularly bad, this brought a crowd to the beaches to watch the proceedings and to lend a hand if necessary.

There was one occasion, while I was watching one of the boaties making a rather difficult landing, when a woman went up to her husband and said, 'How much fish have ye got, Sandy?' Her man turned to her and said, 'Four boxes and a weet backside, woman.'

There have been several wrecks along the coast from Cairnbulg to Rattray Head. The coastguards did great work with the rockets and breechs Buoys, which was a very tricky operation. The Fraserburgh Lifeboat and Cairnbulg coastguards cover the area near St. Combs. The Rattray Head end would be covered by the Rattray coastguards. The older fishermen were very superstitious and you daren't mention pigs, rabbits or salmon whilst on a fishing trip. There was also an old woman in the village considered a witch by the fishermen, and if the yawl fishermen had met her whilst going to a fishing trip, they would have turned back, but I went messages for her and carried water for her and I thought she was a kindly auld wifie and often she gave me a 'bawbee', which she could ill afford but which you daren't give her back. Nellsie's Annie was such a superstitious fish wife. If she wished to exchange fish for a rabbit she daren't mention rabbit and she used to shout across the field, 'Fower (four) legs, ye ken fine fit I mean a R——,' holding up four fingers. The farmer knew well what she meant but liked to tease her. There was an anecdote about two fishermen, who were mending their cod nets at the Cample when this minister on holiday with his two young daughters got into conversation with them about the biblical fishermen. 'Well, lads, you're busy with your nets. I too am a fisherman "of men".' One of the fishermen, having a look at his good-looking daughters, said, 'Well minister, I think you should have pretty good results with bait like that.'

As the yawl fishermen aged, there was nobody to take their place and fishing declined, although some tradesmen did carry out some part-time fishing. The boaties deteriorated and most were broken up.

My mother was in Fraserburgh and waiting at the harbour with my auntie Meggie (Beedie's wife) for the drifter to arrive. My mother wasn't in the least fishing orientated and asked Meggie what the funny boat was at the end of the harbour. Meggie said, 'Eh, Meggens, Maggie Ann, hud yer tongue, folk will think you come fae the Hill o' Mormond, that's nae a boat, that's the pontoon.'

As you will have gathered from what has gone before, fishermen's wives in those days had a pretty hard time, slaving from morning until night and attending their men hand and foot. The fishermen would land, walk away from their yawls, flop down in the fireside chair where their wives pulled off their sea boots, trousers, stockings, drawers, the lot, and often shaved them into the bargain. As young lads we used to sing the following ditty:

> Oh fa' wid be a fisherman's wife
> Tae Gyan wi' a scrubber a creel and a knife
> A deed oot fire and a ravelt bide
> Tae gyan tae the mussels in the mornin.

The fisherfolk used to tramp miles to the mussel beds and dump them in local pools until they were required to bait the lines. The mussels were taken from their shells (sheelen mussels) with a knife and put in a basin until they were baited on to the lines. The lines as they were baited were laid neatly into skulls (baskets), the hooks at the front and the layers separated with paper strips.

John Bruce (Johnny Breecy) was a well-known yawl fisherman. He had engaged young Andra to be his crew-member. Having set their cod nets, Johnny asked Andra to take the bearing location for their nets. Andra: 'Well, Johnny, I mak it that Fite (White) coo (cow) in Corsie's perk on the wast fit o'Mormond.' Johnny almost threw Andra overboard, saying to him, 'Boy, I think you should get a job in Mormond and tether that fite coo on the wye.'

On the way South one of the local drifters was driven into Hull with bad weather. As one of the crew was walking along the docks he saw a load of cattle being loaded on to the cargo boat with derrick and sling. He remarked to the Stevedore, 'Man, that's nae mowze' (not very safe) – Stevedore replied, 'Yes, Sir, they've helluva mouths.'

Fishing

There were yawlies and scaffies and fifies ena
There were zulies, pipe stalkies, richt drifters as weel
But noo their boaties cost thousands o pounds.
Fae Lerwick to Lowestoft richt doon the East side
And roon the wild Pentland and down the West coast
Tae Ireland, and England and Holland as weel
They a hid their season, they a hid their time
Those boaties they followed, the darlings around.
There wis famine and plenty, of siller and fish
There was dumping, restrictions, what will they hae neist.
But far are the curers, the gutters the huts
A thing o the past, for better or worse.
And far are the boaties, and far are the crews
Their passing it was such a terrible wrench

Some of the earlier fishermen were press-ganged. One case was a Wiver
Buchan, who was enticed from his boat to serve in the Napoleonic Wars
and served in the Admiralty boat *Shannon* as a powder monkey. The family boat was named the *Shannon* in memory of this episode. I got this
story from Bruce's Sandy a long time ago. Sandy was a surgeon in
Dundee for many years and has stayed on in Dundee in his retirement. The
fishermen's dress was of a very set pattern. The undervest was known as a
'linner', this consisted of a length of flannel wool usually made by the
women. It was a simple affair, just like a sack with holes for the arms and
head. Our shop sold this flannel for a little over a shilling a yard. Some of
the women might buy a 'seemit', a heavy wool machined vest. The sark
(shirt) was a heavy dark-coloured garment and could withstand heavy
washing treatment. The underpants (drawers) were home knitted from
wheelan worsted (wheelan) and better known as wheelan drawers, the
wool being bought for under a shilling the cut, the cut being the term used
for the wool measurement before the introduction of skeins or ounces.
These drawers were very warm but they were very heavy. During the
winter months after washing them and hanging them out to dry, if they got
frozen they could stand up on their own. The shop sold a manufactured
woollen type of underpants which were referred to as 'Long Johns'. The
overgarment would be a jersey or gansey and these would be home
knitted, usually in a navy blue wool called 'fingering wool', a finer wool
than wheeling. Later on, a different type of jersey became popular, a

speckled grey oiled wool type and this was taken from the trawler-type garment. The trousers were usually of a black or dark brown colour (kerseys). The fly was usually buttoned but some of the fishermen preferred a fold-down front. Another type of top was called a 'barket jumper', this was a cotton garment which could be 'barket' dyed along with the nets.

Sea boots stockings were thigh length, again home knitted in wheeling wool, and were very heavy. They were used by the kids for their Santa Claus stockings. New Year more than Christmas was celebrated by the children, the gifts being oranges, apples, sweets and the inevitable lump of coal. Sea boots were very heavy leather affairs, oil treated and again thigh length, always treated with linseed oil before a fishing season started. Toppers were a small version of leather boot but their length being below the knee and again oil treated. The toppers were also used by the gutting quines. These leather boots were superseded by rubber boots and, when at sea, all this would be topped or covered by oil skins and a souwester, depending on the weather conditions. The yawl fishermen often wore 'oilskin' brecks. The oilskins were all heavily treated with linseed oil and got the usual pre-treatment on the opening of the fishing

Granny Mary at the nets, around 1890.

season. These were formidable garments and could cause chaffing at the wrists and the inevitable salt-water boils. Cuffs were worn on the wrists to alleviate this condition. The shop sold linseed oil and initially the oil-skins. The fishermen also had their go ashore garments, which could be a souped-up version of the trousers and gansey or, depending on their after work activities, might stretch to a blue serge suit and shirt, also with stocker money in pocket. Stocker money was a by-product of the fishing activities, such as fishing while the nets were set or scumming – that is, scooping stray herring spilled over whilst hauling the nets.

The boots or shoes would be given a good rub for the huts' visits, and, of course, the inevitable navy home-knitted socks. A term I often heard was 'brushed boots and empty pockets', meaning no stocker money, a sign of a poor fishing. Another meaning would be pride and poverty.

The firms the shop dealt with for wool and blankets were: Laidlaws & Paton and Baldwins.

The Cample -v- The Camphill

I dinna like the Cample
For the wye that it's spelt
To me, it is the Camphill
For on that camp beside the hill
A those mony lang years ago
The woaded Buchaners dressed in skins
Did wait for their Danish foes
Wi tangles, clubs and muckle steens
Wi sticks and beens and other things
They laid aboot wi sic micht
That they routed these invaders.
Then they sent the bents alicht
That hastened their departure
The weary Danes took tae their heels
And never darkened oor shores again.

Noo if you say the Cample
It hissna got that certain ring
And disna stir the heart ava
It's associated with those baldies
Those boaties fae the Blue Toon
And also fae the Broch

They scoored oor bars and shories
And dragget up the bloomin lot
Till there were nae fishies left
For us to catch wi linies.
Oh that those woaded Buchans
Wi tangles, clubs and steens
Could get among those baldies
As they did to those ancient Danes
A those lang lang years ago.

Fishermen

A fisherman's life it was ever a trauchle
And maest o' th time like a heid-on win
Tae Lerwick, tae Lewis and Yarmouth forbye
It wis redden and shotten and hawlen – Aye hasle
It wis storms and spewen and saut water biles
And a whit for – a mountain o' debt.

A laddie fae skweel on a roch maiden trip
In the gelly he vrocht wi his tied doon pots
I'st a handfae o saut to the big tattie pot
Or a jugfae o' rice tae the man
The crew did torment wi kindly asides
Gweed how he wished he'd stayed on at the skweel.

There was Bella and Gena and Betsy as weel
A watchin the seas bracken ower the pier
The storm twas the worst for mony a year.
At last their boatie was rounding the heid
It was pitching and tossing like some wild thing
But fou wis their laddie and his tied doon pots.

The Reaper (reproduced by kind permission of the Anstruther Fishing Museum).

Car Hiring

This was a service which my father started in the thirties. There were no cars, no ambulances in the village, and in an emergency such as illness there was no means of getting to Aberdeen quickly when anyone had to be hospitalised. Aberdeen was about forty miles from the village. We had a bull-nosed Morris which we did all sorts of things with and which had cost us £120 new.

One day my father said to go to Coral Hill and pick up Mr. Wright and take him to Lonmay station to catch the Fraserburgh/Aberdeen train. I arrived in plenty of time but Mr. Wright (Coral) was rather late in coming out and left me rather short of time. After I got off the side roads, and on to the B road, I put my foot down and was tearing along the road when I felt a tap on my shoulder and the remark from Coral came, 'Noo, Noo, laddie, jist ca canny; I would like to catch the trainie, but better tae miss it than be ower seen intae Hell.' On another trip I had to take a woman to Gamrie (Gardenstown) to a Faith Mission conference and, on arriving in Gamrie, I had difficulty in finding the meeting place and the woman got out of the car and was rushing up and down the Gamrie braes to locate the hall. I caught up with her sitting on a dyke and about ready to pass out. Trying to be helpful, I said I would fetch her a drink. 'Na na, laddie, it's nae a drink I need, but a puckly (little) more breath,' she said. I told her I had found the meeting place, which pleased her, but on arriving at the hall it was discovered she had mistaken the time of the meeting and was just in time to hear the Benediction. However, she was not the least annoyed, being satisfied to see her mission quinies. On this journey, I also met up with George Buchan (Shoddy Love), who had cycled from St. Combs to Gamrie for the conference. He told me he had landed in Macduff and he had been looking for Gamrie on the signposts and only discovered when he landed in Macduff that he should have been looking for Gardenstown. My mother and aunt decided to take Granny Mary on a visit to her old stumping ground, Pennan. At its entrance, Pennan has a very steep brae and Granny would only go if I let her out to walk down the brae. On arriving at the brae, Mother and Aunt restrained her whilst I safely negotiated the brae. She was very upset and consigned the Pennan rocks to fall on me for my behaviour. No amount of pressure would persuade her to go in the car until it was up the hill.

I did some travellers' rounds for a Mr. Cruickshank and a Mr. Duthie, who travelled for groceries from Aberdeen. Mr. Cruickshank was a real old-fashioned gentleman who travelled for George Mellis & Sons (now amalgamated), the wholesale grocers. He was in his seventies when he and I were on this round. I was taking him from the village of Strichen to the Tyrie shop. I had just descended a steep hill and was climbing another, when I thought there was something wrong with the car and intended to stop at the top of the hill to investigate. I never got to the top for a rear wheel came off and the car slumped down on the brake drum. The wheel came running up the hill and bumped into the back of the car. I went down the brae, picked up the hub cap and found a couple of nuts. I was getting ready to try and put the jack under the axle when two farmers came out of the farm opposite (Tyrie Mains). They had a look at the situation and commented, 'Ae, ae, laddie, yer in a bit of trouble but never mind, my laddie, we will lift yer carrie and you push yer wheelie on.' This they did without any bother and Mr. Cruickshank was still sitting in the car. These farmers were the famous Bells of tug-o'-war fame. It is said they used to train for the events by pulling a cart without wheels across a ploughed park. I still come across them, as they play bowls for the Buchan team. I discovered later that my father had been changing a wheel when the phone rang and I was away before he could advise me.

On another trip I narrowly avoided an accident with a runaway pony that had been startled by a backfire. I saw this pony charging down the side road and, if I had braked, the pony and cart would have smashed into the car but, instead of braking, I speeded up and the pony passed by the rear. Incidentally, we used to own this pony but gave it to one of the local farmers – the Buchans at Invernorth.

I have taken patients to and from hospital, relatives to visit dying patients, carried coffins, calves, pigs, even people to jail and people to get baptised, plus funerals and weddings, including a runaway wedding at which I acted as a witness. For both of them it was their second marriage. I also remember the Sheriff's closing remarks to the husband. 'Now see and be good to her as long as you are spared.'

I have several times had to go with my father and relatives to collect mentally disturbed patients from the links, the sea and from home.

Mr. Duthie was the other traveller I used to take round the district and he was of local descent and had relatives in the district. He and his sons carried on a wholesale grocery business in Aberdeen. My day trips amounted to something like 30s. 0d. One Sunday I was asked to take people to the Baptist Church in Peterhead for baptism. Our car was otherwise engaged and my father was going to conduct a service in one of the district churches. Tom Buchan (coal Tom) offered his car but said it wasn't behaving very well, being very jerky as he described it. I got as far as St. Fergus when it started to behave oddly and then smoke started to come through the floor. I drove it into the verge and then went underneath the car to find the battery cable resting on the exhaust and burning as well as earthing. I pulled it away and got some material to insulate it and tie it away from the exhaust. The clients described it as the Devil's last fling. Well, there might have been an inferno if I hadn't caught it in time. Coal Tom said his car was as good as new. It was one of the earliest Rovers.

I used to deliver the weekly stores to some of the local drifters. This was on a Monday morning. I also collected many of the singers and other performers for the local concerts. Once while I was on a trip and was on my way home, when this terrible wind and snow storm got up in no time at all, there were nine inches of snow on the ground. I was making heavy weather of it when, about two miles from home, I saw this woman with a bike sitting at the bottom of the hill. I couldn't stop or I wouldn't have got started again. I went back to the woman, put her bike over the fence and led her exhausted to the car. She couldn't talk for some time and said she had thought that I was going to abandon her. I explained the position, saying I had already stuck and also that I had to alter my route. I took her to her father's house in the village where he thanked me. I collected her the next morning and took her to her bike; the storm had died down but there wasn't another mark on the snow. I am sure that if I hadn't come along that night she would have been a casualty of the weather.

On another occasion I was driving home with a male passenger beside me when we approached an assortment of roadworks, lorries and work-men. I slowed down at the start of the group and the watchman waved me on. There must have been a length of about thirty yards of single track road due to this working party, and right at the very end of the line was a road roller and driver. Just as I approached the roller, the driver jumped into the middle of the road with his back to me. I swerved the car, ran up the bank verge, nearly upsetting the car. Luckily, I just caught the edge of his flying jacket and turned him round. There was a goods lorry waiting for me to come out of the single track and the driver came out of his cab and went for the roller driver, letting him know how lucky he was and that he deserved to be killed for such stupid behaviour. The driver of the road roller was most apologetic and said he wasn't hurt and that there would be no more said about it. The lorry driver gave me his name and said that if there were any further developments he would be a witness in my defence. I never heard anything further. My passenger was more shaken that I was and said it was a good job he hadn't been driving.

Petrol at this time was 1s. 3d. a gallon, paraffin was 9d. and there were no automatic wipers, no heaters and some cars had carbide lamps, although our Morris had electric lights. Some cars had no automatic starters and all had starting handles.

A local laird went down South to purchase a Rolls Royce. The Salesman was giving the usual patter to the Laird and his chauffeur about all the good points and the magnificence of the car, but the Lairdie wasn't to be taken in by all the propaganda. 'Well, salesman, if the automobile is all that good, why has it got a starting handle?' The salesman, not to be outdone, replied 'Sir, I take it you do take a bath – and have you seen a little hole in your stomach [belly button] – and do you ever use it?' The laird replied, 'No.' 'Well, Sir, the same applies to the starter handle, it's just there in case.'

There were no petrol pumps, petrol was obtained from the paraffin delivery lorries in two-gallon tins. There were no garages and no motor mechanics and most of the time minor repairs were do-it-yourself jobs. Tachy (Strachan), although not a qualified mechanic, used to do odd jobs on the initial cars. The first car I owned cost me £25 and I sold it to Tachy for £5. This car was a little Austin Seven two-seater sports car, which I used to fly about in and return home to St. Combs. One of the lads made up a little ditty about it.

'Davie's got a little car, he broke the thirty mile, and now he reads some 'Dixon Hawks' to spend the time in jyle.'

Although it was classed as a sports car, it was no speedster but served its purpose. After my father's death, my mother asked me to get rid of it. I got a second-hand Ford for £40.

Car Hiring

At the turn of the century
The car was a' sae strange

But in the nineteen twenties
They weren't quite so rare,
There was Crimond's Eddie Burnett
Lonmay hid Dooey Reid
They plied their cars for hire
Aroon the countryside.

Syne Patty got a Morris car
It did sae mony different things
Like takin' calvies tae the market.
It took fermers there as well.
It was also used for waddens,
For funerals and for births,
For baptisms and hospitals,
Even some it took to jyle.

Anither time I went
Tae pick this mannie up
He wis sae late in comin oot
That I wis forced to rush
He tappit on my shewder
Said, 'Laddie, jist ca' canny
It's better that we miss the train,
I'm nae ready for my makker.'

Eats and Meats

In earlier times, apart from walks and feast days (weddings, funerals), most meals were very simple affairs. Soups were all homemade, no tinned soups in those days; even when they did appear, my granny used to refer to tin food as the lazy housewife's meat. The broth pot was very seldom out of use, being used for broth, tattie, lentil, fish, oxtail, skink, rice and various other concoctions. A bone or a cheap cut of meat (3d. or 6d. worth) was used for the stock pot, pease meal and neep brose, especially in the cottar hooses roon aboot. When the butcher's 'Auntie Jeannie' made neep brose, there was always a bowlful sent up for my father. The standard Sunday meal would be broth and beef and dumpling. Sowens supped with syrup; I have seen several men in our house when my mother made sowens, supping up their sowens with great delight. Its use died out in the district in the 1930s and I don't suppose anyone in the village makes it now or has even heard of it. It was made from sids – cereal husks. Fresh herring well coated with oatmeal with a quort (quarter) o' bread and fresh quintry (country) butter and eaten with new Buchan tatties (Boothby Fare). To get their winter tatties some villagers used to hire a drill of tatties from a local farmer (Cairnglass). The farmer prepared the drill and the villagers planted the tatties and the farmer covered them up. In the autumn when the tatties were ready, the farmer unearthed them and the village renter gathered them up and put them in sacks. The villagers also went tattie picking at nearby farms such as Cairnglass, Corskelly, Quarryhill, Woodhead, Middleton, Netherton, Coralhill, etc.

Occasionally, a Sunday hen would be on the menu, this being cooked along with the broth – the hen being stuffed with oatmeal, suet, onions and seasoning. Oatmeal would be purchased in bulk and stored in a barrel. This store resulted in the often used wedding telegram: 'May the meal in your girnal never rin deen.' The oatmeal was used for porridge, oatcakes, gruel, loafies, scones, pancakes, etc. A dumplin was made with flour, suet, sugar, raisins, currants, spices, milk, and these were mixed together and tied in a clout (cloth) and boiled along with the broth; this had the advantage of sweetening the broth, it was very nice.

A loafie, as my granny called it, was made with similar ingredients but with different quantities; and instead of being put in the broth pot it was pressed into what was called a kettle, a three-legged metal cast iron pot with a lid which was hung over the fire on the swye, the swye hooks and chain adjusting the pot height.

Most cooking utensils were made of cast iron and were very durable – pots, kettles, frying pans, girdles. Oatcakes were made in large amounts and stored in barrels.

The drifters were supplied with large amounts of oatcakes and a new herring barrel was supplied to the woman or women who were to bake the oatcakes. Some boats would ask for a particular woman to bake their oatcakes. My Uncle Beedie always asked Isa Ann to bake his supply. I used to take down a stone of oatmeal and a pound of fat. Isa Ann (Mrs. Strachan) spent her day baking and packing the barrel.

Fish was eaten in large quantities – herring, cod, saithe, haddock, whiting, all fresh or smoked. Flat fish from the smaalins were also used, they being the smaller ones which were unsuitable for market. A barrel of salt herring was in most fishermen's outhouses, the barrel being prepared when the herring were at their best before spanning. They were eaten from newspapers along with tatties in their skins.

Potted heid was also made. A cow's head was bought from the butcher and cooked in the wash-house boiler, seasoned and put into bowls. 'Titt' (Mrs. Buchan) of Seafield View used to make large amounts and the villagers used to take their bowls up to her house the night before, when they heard that she was to be making potted heid. She filled your bowl and it cost around 6d. I often took up a bowlie from my granny to Titt's.

There were two dairies in the village – James Buchan (Dairy Jim) and his farm was Cairnglass and they supplied the milk which was served from the Dairy in Mid Street by their daughter Margaret (Diry Marget) at a penny a pint. The other dairy was in Bridge Street (Athurie's Diry) it was run by his wife Annie Crookie, who never ventured far from home and was a very hard-working woman. Robertson took it over later.

As there was no running water in the village, water for drinking and cooking had to be carried from two wells by pails and yoke. One well was on the north side of the village in the Charleston direction and was known as the Miller's (Mulert's) Well and the Brick Well on the south side. Two pails of water carried by the yoke, was known as a 'fracht'. Common cereals used were: rice, sago, tapioca; these were mixed with other ingredients like rice and raisins, sago and apples, prunes, figs, dates. Corned beef came in later (Granny – 'lazy wife's meat').

A branner (brander) was a much-used cooking utensil. This was a single or double grid iron which was used for roasting fish, meat, cheese, sausages, potatoes, etc. The fire was stoked up and blown with a bellows so that the coals glowed red, the brander was put on top and the article to be cooked put on the brander. Speldings (dry whitings) were cooked in this way.

Eggs were 9d. a dozen, wild birds' eggs were used, e.g. lapwing's, tern's, crow's – on a seasonal basis. Fowl eggs were preserved for the winter. These were placed in a large earthenware tub and a preservative such as waterglass or keepeg was used. These eggs kept well until the Spring when the eggs would become more plentiful. There were no battery hens in those days, all were free range (rinnen aboot hens).

Rabbits were caught and poached, these being stewed or used to make soup. A rabbit may have cost about 9d. or 1s. 0d., depending where it was obtained, the skin was usually exchanged for a bowl or plate from the travelling ragman (Matheson's cairt).

When things were low, tatties and dip were the meal of the day. This was boiled tatties which you dipped in the salt. Chappet tatties had the addition of chives or maybe a little flaked yellow fish.

Saps was made with boiled milk and all the old hard bread thrown into it with some sugar and perhaps a handful of raisins. There was, of course, the Buchan standby – mince and tatties. Skirly and tatties: Skirly was made with oatmeal, onions and seasoning. Stovies: this was tatties with meat scraps and some fat. Hairy tatties: the hard fish which had been cured and dried over the summer season, were used to make this meal. The hard fish were boiled until soft, drained and flaked up and mixed with a little butter. The tatties were boiled chappet (mashed) and the two were mixed together. The mixture could be put in a dish and browned on top or eaten as mashed; usually a glass of milk would be drunk along with this meal.

Yirned milk curds: this brings to mind a story. I was having water works problems at the time and had to supply a specimen for tests. I was also taking a liquid medicine. I put my urine sample in a clean bottle, in an out of the way place in the cupboard, and the medicine in a handy place. I went to the cupboard and poured what I thought was the medicine into the glass. I just took a little sip and it was horrible. I thought it was the urine sample, but it was still in its place. Unbeknown to me, Eleanor, the girl, had been using rennet and had put it where my medicine was. I chased Eleanor out of the house in case she used the urine for the curds. I told the doctor about it and he had a good laugh in case I used the rennet for a sample.

In the old days, especially during the winter months, cooking had to be done by the light of an oil lamp (a cruisie); this was a cast iron dish with a hook hanger at one end and a spout at the other, where dried reeds were placed as the wick. The oil used was fish oil and it was a very smoky affair. There were candles, paraffin lamps in single and double and round wick form, Aladdin, Tilley and carbide lamps. The Aladdin and Tilley lamps used a mantle. This is an Aladdin lamp tale about a fisherman who had just acquired an Aladdin lamp and was using it as he repaired his nets, which had been torn during the South fishing. He had a friend helping him and they had finished their night's work. He showed his friend downstairs to the door and said to his helper, 'Hiv ye got yer feet, Sandy? Guid nicht tae ye, I'll see ye the morn.' Forgetting he was using the Aladdin, he gave the lamp an almighty blow and blew the mantle to bits.

A chip shop started in the village, the chips being cooked in the wash boiler, and they were really good. The chip shop was run by Leeby Ann (Strachan) and her father Jeemsie (Bumble). The chip shop was in a little end house and sometimes became rather crowded with kids waiting for their pennyworth of chips. On this day 'Jeemsie' spied this lad hanging about for a long time and addressed him as follows: 'Hiv ye gotten yer maet, hiv ye geen Leeby Ann yer penny? Weel lidder.' Translated, this would be, 'Have you given Elizabeth Ann your penny after getting your chips? Now hurry along.'

Large amounts of home-made jams were prepared during the summer months. There wasn't a great deal of fruit grown in the village, it being too exposed to the salt breezes. The fruit was usually obtained from farmers who came to the village with their carts filled with berries, or the fishwives would barter their fish for fruit. Most houses had a large berry pan. My parents had a very large pan and made jam for the house and the shop. I always remember I had to put a half crown (2s. 6d.) at the bottom of the pan, which was supposed to stop burning the fruit. Blackcurrants and gooseberries were often used as they gave a bigger output per pound. Dilse (Dulse) was a seaweed which could be eaten raw, or roasted by running a hot poker over it, or by roasting it on the brander. Lobsters, crabs (partens), especially partens, were a seasonal dish, the large toes being taken to school for a playtime piece. Grandfather West was a real expert at preparing shellfish for a meal.

As I have said before, there was no running water in the village. I often had to carry water for my granny. She stayed nearer the Mulert's Well which had a soft water, but she preferred her drinking water to come from the Brick Wall which had a hard water. This well was nearer our own house but further away from 'Auchmedden', my granny's house. Granny's instructions were, 'Noo, Davie, I want Brick Wall water, go straight there, and straight back – nae half wye hooses and dinna speak tae ony bairns on the wye.' My payment was, 'Davie, when I'm awa, there's a silk wiscut [waistcoat] in the kist [trunk] the claeth [cloth] wis bocht in Bombay and it was mayed [made] in Steenhive [Stonehaven] and it's yours.' Some years later when granny was awa I got it from an aunt, have never worn it, but still have it. It must be well over 100 years old.

The arrival of water and drainage in the thirties was a great boon to the village, for drinking water had to be carefully used. Rain water from the roof, stored in barrels or tanks, was used for washing. This had also to be used carefully during dry spells as the bowies (barrels) were apt to run dry. It was said that one old person wouldn't drink the tap water until many months after it had been installed, still carrying his drinking water from the well. He maintained the pipes weren't clean. It was said that when he got electricity he only used it to let him see to light his paraffin lamp.

The Brick Wall

Puir auld wallie ye man be lonesome
And man miss the village folkies
That came to you throwe rain and shine
To fill their pails wi guid fresh water.
Maest o' them hive worn awa
The trackie noo is a grown ower.
Many a time I have cursed you
When I hid tae walk that nerra trackie
Wi yoke and pails – a fracht o'water.
That yokie did hurt when I wanted tae play
And made me pech when I climbed a brae.
That's a'forgotten as you get aulder.
Puir wallie ye man be jist awfa lonesome.
A mannie named Morgan fae Aberdeen

Came tae the toon and sealed yer fate
Wi picks and shovels and local labour
Dug trenchies a ower fae heed tae fit
The toonie streets hid niver seen
The likes o' it since time began
That mannie laid pipes and drains aroon
And gave us water tae a' oor hoosies
Peer wallie ye must hae wondered
Fit hid come ower a'yer folkies.
The water fae the hoosie pipies
It didna taste the same as yours
And mony o' yer far flung folkies
Would like to drink a suppie O't
And walk along that grown ower trackie
But someday seen a clever mannie
May come and bottle up yer waters
And sell it in the supermarkets
The best of a' the mineral waters.

Eating Habits

The old folkies maet, wis gie simple fare
An made to fill a' hantle o' moos
A lot o' tatties, a lot o' fish
As well as the 'chepper' cuts o' beef
A coo's heid in the biler,
The outcome was large
A lot o' bowls o' fine potted heid
A barrel or twa of guid saut herrin
They made ye drink, this fooed ye up
An ye didna need much for the rest o' the day
There were hairy tatties wi a gless o' milk
Or skirlie or stovies wi hame made breed
But on peerer days, it wis tatties and dip
An how much better were hame made mealies
A fry o fresh herrin just oot o' the sea
And dichted a ower wi guid Buchan meal
This, it wis said, was Boothby's delight
But Sunday it wis that wee bitty special
Wi dumplin' an broth for a' in the hoose.

During the war when rationing was in force, having been introduced by Lord Woolton, it was pretty hard on the older folk. Jimmy used to come in and get his meagre rations and it was always his moan, 'I'll bet Lord Wulten's nae sitten doon tae this – this widnae feed a moose aleen a man. There a moose in my hoose and I canna spare a bitty o' my cheese ration to bait the trap.'

A butcher rationing tale: 'I'm needin thripence worth o' liver tae the cat and nae pipies int cause my fadder disna like pipies [rough pieces].'

'A 3d. been and dinna bother scrapen off the beef on't.'

Eating times were your brakfest (breakfast), denner (dinner) about one o'clock and your tae (tea) about six o'clock, then you had a cup of tae before bedtime. My Uncle David and his wife Nellie, having been abroad, had their main meal at night. This was of great concern to Granny. 'Fit wye can Davie an his wife nae be like ither folk, they hiv their denner at nicht inside o' denner time. They gin ower the braes and gither poddick steels (mushrooms) and fry them wi their maet. It's a wunner they're nae pooshint [poisoned].'

This is the story of one man's meat being another man's poison. Jeannie Lonnie had some English visitors staying with her who were highly delighted eating the livers and roes from herring. They couldn't get enough of the soft roes, as they called them. 'Guid sakes,' says she.

I used to enjoy fish soup when made by my mother but, whilst I was in the Strichen isolation hospital with scarlet fever, I went right off it, for when I was handed my fish soup, there were two fish eyes staring at me from the bowl – no more fish soup for me for a long time. I've heard sheep eyes are an eastern delicacy but never heard any mention of fish eyes. Sometimes we did use them as bait for catching pirries (small fish). Lots of the fish that are sold and eaten nowadays were discarded or used as crab bait such as dog fish, monk, campers, eels, freshwater flukies, etc.

I remember my father's remarks when I used to turn up my nose at any food. 'Well, laddie, ye'll tak it afore it taks you. Ye can tak a dish o' want next time.'

The Family

Granny Mary (Onack's Mary) was my mother's mother and was a real character and would have gone through fire and water in her earlier days, unlike her husband Andrew West (Wast), who was a quiet, staid and more intellectual person than his wife. He always addressed his wife as Mrs. (Mistress). When they were married they started their married life in the hamlet of Pennan near the Banffshire border. Wast was engaged plying his boat *The Lively* up and down the coast. Mary Buchan (Onack's Mary) didn't like Pennan, it being too small for her restless spirit, so during one of her husband's trips, she up-tailed (left) with her first born on her back, and walked all the way to St. Combs. She got her way, as she most often did, the two of them setting up house at 'Auchmedden' on Braeheads. The name 'Auchmedden' was named after an area near Pennan. The meaning of Auchmedden was middle meadow. Most of the families in those days were large and my grandparents were no exception.

A rundown on the family is as follows.

Mary Christina West (Teenie) was the first born who lived until she was ninety-nine and she married John Trail who owned a booksellers and newspaper business in Fraserburgh, the name is still in use today. All your school books were obtained from the shop. Teenie became a Fraserburgh town councillor and later a Baillie, and she inherited a lot of her mother characteristics and was a real go ahead person. She and my mother were somewhat similar in facial appearance and this brings to mind a story. My mother was in Fraserburgh and met an ex-St. Combs woman who asked if she was Teenie and, when my mother replied in the negative, the woman said she somehow thought that because 'Teenie's aye sae grand buckled' (dressed).

Andrew West (Beedie), the second born, also known to his crew as 'Full Butt'. He was a very successful fisherman and was for a time in the

78

Grandfather, Andrew West.

Grandmother, Mary West (née Buchan).

fish-curing business as well. He set up house in Fraserburgh and married a Portknockie woman called Meggie. Charles West (Yahoo) was third in line and was a joiner and carpenter and he was never robust. His wife died leaving him with three children, two boys and a girl. Granny brought up the two boys as her own, the girl being brought up by her aunt on her mother's side. David Buchan West (Pret) qualified as a chemist and went abroad and set up a business in Port Elizabeth in South Africa. I am named after him.

I have related one episode about David and Minnie and here is another he related to me about his business in South Africa. He made up and sold a lot of his own medicines like West's corn cure, hand creams and talcs. On this occasion, it was hair restorer. He obtained the model of a man's bust and head, he took off the crown of the head and inserted a container with some soil and grass seed. He put a notice alongside the model saying, **'Come back next week and see what Wests restorer can do.'** In a few days the grass was growing and there was a crowd outside with heads as bald as coots that no amount of hair restorer would have made any difference to. Business was brisk and some of the natives were chatting away in their native tongues. In the shop at the time was Betsy, who had just arrived from St. Combs and was rather overcome by all this chatter,

Family.

and, not understanding a word, she said to David (Pret) – 'Peer things, Davie, it's an awfa peety (pity) they canna speak like ither folk.'

Maggie Ann, my mother, was the village Postmistress for many years. She was also President of the British women in the village (B.W.T.A) and other stalwarts of the Temperance Association were Duncan's Nan and Jeannie Lonnie. The B.W.T.A. has now been disbanded locally and nationally. She organised outings for the Association and on one of the outings this worthy was parading about the town they were visiting and greeting everybody with the remark, 'Fine day, man, and a huntle o' folk',

Family.

imagining that everybody knew about their trip. Another woman, being handed a salad for her lunch, remarked, 'Na, na, quinie, that's nae mine, I dinna want yer rabbit's maet.'

Alex West (Sandy) spent most of his time at sea on cargo liners and he was always a bit of a wanderer, coming and going without due warning.

Family.

He stopped off in Australia and South Africa to visit his sister and brother. Sometimes he worked there before picking up another ship. He got malaria during these trips. He eventually married late and settled down in Auchmedden. Jessie West (Minnie Jessie), a name she didn't like, qualified as a teacher, teaching at various locations in Scotland but coming home on holidays fairly often. She married a banker, and with her family spent holidays at Auchmedden. Her three sons named Granny Mary 'Granny Noo Noo' because when they got rather boisterous, she would say 'Noo, noo, watch fit yer daen.' The eldest of the boys was inclined to let others take advantage of him and Granny would say, 'Davie, that boyicky's nae feel, he's just glaiket – gowket fessen up. He's like Toshie's lemonade' (light).

John Clark West (Clark) spent some time abroad in Australia and Africa and also at the herring fishing but he finally settled and spent his time in the freshing trade, i.e. buying the early herring catch, salting and icing them and transporting them to the South Market. He married Betsy Taylor from Broadsea (Fraserburgh) who worked for my parents. Their daughter became almost a sister as she spent so much time at our home.

Jemima West I didn't know very well. She married a local lad – a Buchan (Rogue) and emigrated to Sydney Australia (Botany). They didn't communicate a lot with St. Combs and never visited the village. Number Ten was named Forrest (Forrestie) after the local minister and he died in infancy. Forrest was the local minister for many years and he lived in the manse at Lonmay. He wrote a book about Buchan and carried out research into the early church in the district. He presented a Bible as a wedding present to my father in 1908 and I still have it in the house. Dr. Forrest died in 1914.

One strange thing about the family was that most of them died with lung trouble or cancer of some sort.

My paternal grandparents I didn't know – Pet's Peter and Meg. They died when I was an infant but, from what I can gather from villagers, they were highly thought of and helped out a lot of the villagers financially. Their family was: Andrew Buchan (Andy) the eldest son and he trained locally as a baker and emigrated to America (Boston) where he carried on in the bakery trade. The family visited St. Combs to stay with his wife's parents. He married Sailor's Kirsten (Buchan). In fact, their eldest son stayed in the village and went to school in the village. He later returned to Boston. He was in the American Navy during the war and when he was in this country called to see my mother, who gave him a pair of my many locally knitted socks. He was named after his father and was known locally as Yank.

Lizzie Buchan (Lizzie Watt) was the eldest daughter and married and settled in the village from which she never strayed. She was a very quiet person and was seldom seen without her knitting. She knitted socks and jerseys for her grandchildren. She was widowed early.

Peter Buchan (Pet's Peter's Patty) known as (Patty) was the third and my father. He married Maggie Ann West, who was the village Postmistress at the time. The Post Office was situated across the road at 7½ Mid Street. My father's ambition was to be a joiner and emigrate to New Zealand, something he never achieved as he had to take over the business when his father retired.

Alex Buchan (Sandy), the youngest child, contracted meningitis when very young and this left him deaf and dumb. He trained as a tailor and married outwith the village and settled in Aberdeen. He didn't visit the village very often.

Margaret Buchan (Mugsie) was the younger daughter and she married James Buchan (Jemky) or Gick's Jim. He was a part owner of the drifter *Ocean Searcher* along with his elder brother John (John Gick or Mackie) and George Buchan (Torry Dody).

My paternal grandparents settled in Seaview and Mugsie and Jimky settled there. They had no family but adopted Mugsie's niece Maggie (Mugsie's Maggie) a daughter of her brother (Sandy Dummy). I had more contact with Auntie Maggie than with my other paternal relations and used to visit often as a nipper. My maternal grandfather was a staunch Tory whilst Pet's Peter was a Liberal. I am told they had some heated debates and attended the hecklings meetings to air their views. The heckling meetings were held in the Kirky and, as a whole, would have been more left than right wing orientated. My father was also a Liberal in the early days and Labour adherents were few and far between. Mr. Martin (Liberal) was the local hero until Bob Boothby came on the scene. Granny Mary wasn't interested in politics and just went along with her husband's views.

She was always dishing out advice such as when she considered someone was marrying above their station.

'Keep among cats o' yer ane kine and yer kittlins will be like ye.'
'A bonny bride is seen busket.'
'Its nae loss that a freen gets.'
'Set a stout hert tae a stey brae.'

'A heep aheen a birn.' (coals to Newcastle)
'Dinna be teen in wi a bonny facie.'
'Can she bake, can she sew, can she make a moufie o maet then had siccar.'
'There's nae feel like an auld feel.'
'He's licht, like Toshie lemonade.'
'He's nae feel, he's jist gowket fissen up.'
'Aye, he's been amongst the craws ena.'
'Gweed gear gings into sma buik.'
'There's ower muckle o him tae be aricht at aye time.'

Some of these sayings were often used but some I haven't heard so often.

The last one I heard her quote when I said that so and so was ill, this person being a large man, she meaning to say that he had such a big body that he had more of him to go wrong than if he were little. 'Gweed gear into sma buik,' she used to apply to myself. I was always rather small for my age, and she used to say, 'Niver mind, Davie, gweed gear gings into sma buik.' There were others which she used but I think they have gone into disuse. More village sayings later. When I was young I used to be delegated to go across and sleep at Auchmedden in what was called a box bed. I didn't care for it very much as it was too warm and too far off the ground. A 'caff seck' was used in place of a mattress, similar to that used in the boats. The caff (chaff) was obtained from a farmer when he threshed his grain at the end of the harvest.

Granny was on her own for some time before my uncle Sandy and his wife Tine (Christine) moved into Auchmedden. My mother was the only one of her family that remained in the village for all of Granny's life and I had to go there pretty frequently to see how she was getting on. My cousin had left his gramophone with Granny when he left the village, leaving the sea to take up work as an optician in London. I used to go over and play the gramophone sometimes on a Sunday. When she used to want the gramophone to be played she used to say, 'Davie will ye play the thingie?'. The tunes available for the 'thingie' were such as 'I belong to Glasgow' – 'I'm 94 this morning', others of Will Fyffe, Harry Gordon and Harry Lauder tunes. As a peace offering, 'The old rugged cross'. She would then finish by saying, 'Dinna tell yer father noo.' The half hoose, which was occupied for a time, was now used to store coal, peat and sticks. It was also used for cooking certain things as it had a swye. On the storage side of this outhouse, she used to sprinkle dry sand from the beach. This was swept up frequently and fresh sand sprinkled around.

This was another duty I sometimes did, carrying sand for the half hoose. This was a throw back to the older times when houses were unfloored. Sweeping the floor meant sweeping up the silver sand from the floor and sprinkling clean sand down on the floor again. She had a garden at the side and back. 'Will ye gie the gerden a redd-up, Davie?' The garden was rather exposed and wasn't very productive.

Patsy and Ellie lived at the back and Ellie used to go in to see her and let us know how she was.

My maternal grandfather (Wast) was a big man and suffered from asthma. He seemed to get some relief when going out to sea. There was always a smell of asthma cure. This was burned and the smoke given off inhaled. He used to smoke asthma cigarettes as well. The cure names were Potters and Hinksmans, there was also a coal tar solution which was heated by a small lamp and inhaled. I personally used cures as well. I suffered from asthma from the age of six or seven years but I found relief when going inland, it left me in my twenties. I was on an army exercise in very inclement weather and was suffering from asthma at the time; it left me during the exercise and I've never had it since, whether by the conditions or my age is open for debate.

Further, as I said, I seemed to get relief when going inland. On this occasion I was pretty bad and my mother took me up to a farm near Alford (Annfield). I used to run about fishing in the burn and climbing nearby hills. One day the farmer was working in the fields taking in his crop of barley. I was running about and in my way supposed to be helping with the leading, when I saw a wasp going into a hole in the ground and I poked a stick in the hole and the wasps came swarming out, stinging everybody around, including the horse which bolted. I was particularly badly stung and bawling my head off and, when I was taken home and stripped, the wasps were everywhere and I was in a bad way. I went into a sort of coma and I think it was bicarbonate of soda they applied and made me drink as well.

It must have been forty years later when my brother was working near Alford (Annfield) when he got talking to a farmer and mentioned that his name was Buchan. The farmer asked if he was from St. Combs and got stung by wasps. My brother informed him that it was his younger brother and that he was still on the go. It was a long while before I got over my fear of wasps and I am still very careful when dealing with them.

Both my brother and I have long names. My brother's name is Sylvester Davidson Fairweather Buchan, whilst my name is David Sandys Clark Buchan. Granny said that it was a case of trying to feed too many dogs with the one bone.

As I have already mentioned, my mother was associated with the B.W.T.A. and was the President for many years. On her twenty-five years' anniversary, she was presented with a gift of a coffee percolator. My Granny said, 'Davie, fits that they've geen yer midder. I thocht that was a thing for bringen oot chuckens.' (incubator).

This story relates to a christening:

The minister addressed the mother: 'Please hold up the child.' Mother held it up and said, 'I'll seen hod it up, I'll hod it up though it wis a little horsie's calfie.' Make what you like of that. That tale was given to me by Jeannie Lonnie.

I mentioned Jemky, John Gick and Torry Dody. These three were stalwarts of the local choir and because of this they were invited by Moultrie Kelsall, a B.B.C. producer, to participate in a local songs programme. They sang various songs, namely: Tar the Yawl, Buchanness Tatties, Peterheid Herren. They were renumerated to the extent of five guineas.

Johnny came into the shop and asked for a paper and two stamps and, in a short time, he was back for another two stamps and a bag of sugar. He then stuck the two stamps on to the bag of sugar. I asked him why he did that. 'Well, they winna blaw awa this time.'

A certain woman was leaving the village for good and asked us to take her cat. It was a large ginger tom and we had had it for a few months when it disappeared. After a couple of days we thought it had come to grief. On the third night, about two o'clock in the morning, I was awakened by the cat howling at the door and the rattling of something on the foot grating. I went downstairs and, on opening the door, there was the cat with a rabbit trap on his foot. I released the trap and carried him inside and fed him. I thought he would never stop feeding. I washed and disinfected his foot and laid him in his bed. After a few days he made a complete recovery. He must have dragged the trap for more than a mile. Whether he had been released or dragged out the trap is unknown.

My Folkies

My Granny on my mither's side
Was kent as Granny Mary
She had a huntle bonny bairns
And slaved from morn til nicht
She washed and scrubbed for them aa
Till they did leave the nestie

I used to rin her errins
Wi a tanner in a cloot
And kerry water fae the walls
Chap her sticks and kerry san
And sometimes she wid gie me
A pancake or a scone

I didna ken my father's folk
As I was far too young
But as far as I can gather
They did a lot of good
They left their shop and settled
On the other side of toon

Sometimes I gid ower the wye
To see my auntie Maggie
She gid tae me, a plate o soup
In a yalla and gowden dishy
And I was made to sup it clean
To see the catty on the bottom

Now all have gone to pastures new
And few of us remember
Our time too is running out
No more, no more remembered

Patty and Maggie Ann

Patty (Pet's Peter's Patty) was my father, the son of Pet's Peter and which was shortened to Patty, sometimes known as Post Office Patty to distinguish him from his school chum Butcher Patty.

Maggie Ann, my mother, was the daughter of Andrew West (Wast) and Mary Buchan (Onack's Mary).

They were both born in the village and were both schooled there. They were married in the 'Ban-Car' Hotel (which is still on the go) by Dr. Forrest in February 1908 and I was born on January 1914. In 1908 the Post Office was in 7½ Mid Street across the road from my father's shop, and when they married the Post Office was integrated with the shop at No. 11 East Street. He stocked all manners of foods and goods and had a horse-drawn van that went all round the country district, driven by A. Strachan (Baker Andy). Quarrie's Pat also did various jobs but he died suddenly whilst he was carrying danders (train cinders) to cover the street from 11 East Street to the High Street. Patty was made a J.P. (Justice of the Peace). This was a great boon to the village for he was able to certify papers, pensions, etc. On my father's death my mother became a J.P. My father was very keen on first aid and was quite an expert and dealt with a lot of breaks, bruises and burns. Most of the villagers would consult my father before calling the doctor. He got a lot of practice from my brother and I, as we were always getting into scrapes of one sort or another. Our house was often like a casualty station. I remember one time I had got my head opened with a golf club and he was cleaning and dressing my head, when a mother came in with her son who had got a hook in his head. After this, another woman came in and asked if he could come down to her house because her mother had fainted. The Crimond Doctor Reid, who attended my father's funeral, spoke to me and said how much he would

Maggie Ann Buchan and Patty Buchan.

miss him and thanked me for all the help he had given over the years, as he had saved him many journeys.

He conducted religious services in a hall at 11 East Street, which was to be a garage. Some of the locals provided a sign and called it the 'Bethel'. Later, when this building deteriorated, and became too small, he erected a new Bethel in Church Street where he conducted his services and also arranged for various other speakers to take part from all over the world. I remember one especially, who was an Armenian who had been driven out of his homeland by Turks. His name was Bogus Arton and he spoke several times in the Bethel. The Faith Mission Pilgrims were regular visitors and the two I remember most were Belford and Cottrel. They were successful in recruiting two girls from the village, Chrissie Bruce (John Breecy's daughter) and Divina Buchan (Buck's daughter). They also got two from the other villages, Katie May and Betsy Duthie. My father conducted many funeral services and helped several financially, also taking a share interest in some of the boats. He stood in on many occasions for ministers going on holiday or due to illness and he was very friendly with Jim Forrest, Superintendent of the Peterhead Fishermen's Mission (R.N.M.D.F.), also the mission in Aberdeen (R.N.M.D.F.). Mr. Crocket was Superintendent.

Jim Forrest preached at the Peterhead Prison and my father went there with him sometimes.

Another of my father's friends was a Mr. Towns, who used to be a minister at Insch and later became superintendent of the Soldiers' Home at Barry Camp, Carnoustie.

My father sometimes went down to Barry to help him out and help with the services. A story I heard Mr. Towns relate was about this young minister who was rather pompous and proud of his preaching ability. He asked Mr. Towns, who had been sitting in the congregation, what he thought of his sermon. 'Weel, laddie, in the first place, you read it, in the second place you didn't read it very well and in the third place, it wasn't worth reading.'

Another story concerns a minister who was forever shifting. Mr. Town said that he was like the cottars' hens. By this he was referring to older times: when cottars shifted they always tied the legs of their hens and it was said that some shifted so often that, when the hens heard a lorry approach, they got on their backs to have their legs tied.

Mr. Towns retired and, with his wife Maggie Towns, opened a boarding house in Aberdeen. My father and mother were regular visitors and I lodged there many times during my stays in Aberdeen.

My father had a breakdown due to the strain of his business and other activities, from which he recovered. He suffered from a heart condition and on the day he was killed he went to Banff to pick up his daughter-in-law and grandchild. They had been spending a holiday with her mother and were returning to Aberdeen. They had an accident at Whiterashes (1938) near Straloch Farm, and he was killed outright and the little girl died shortly afterwards. My sister-in-law was seriously hurt and spent a long time in hospital. At the time of the crash my brother was on his way back from Balmoral Castle, where he had been the resident telephone engineer during the King's holiday (George VI). He just arrived in time to be confronted with the tragic news. I was working in Huntly as a telephone engineer and had just had my tea and gone for a haircut when I was informed about the accident. I returned to St. Combs right away. I obtained a transfer to Peterhead later and was able to return home at night and help out in the shop.

My mother decided to keep on the shop and Janet Strachan (Inverallochy P.O.) very kindly came back to help out on a temporary basis. Irene Greig had been helping in the house and she took over in the shop when Janet left. This was a very trying time for my mother but, with all the moral support she got, she eventually got over it.

My father's funeral was one of the biggest the village has ever seen. The service was held in the Bethel and many of his friends were there to conduct the service. His grandchild was buried along with him in Lonmay cemetery.

My mother took over the office duties again, although things had changed a bit. My mother tells the story about Geordie Breecy of 4 High Street – that's where she started as Postmistress. Geordie kept hens, which he found were not very profitable. They had either been killed, eaten or died off so that, when Geordie was asked about his hens, it was always the same reply: 'Jist a deed loss.' This led to the local saying that any venture which did not succeed was like Geordie Breecy's hens – jist a deed loss.

Geordie was a real character. The local gamekeeper had caught him poaching rabbits and threatened to take him to court. Geordie turned to the Keeper and said, 'Weel, weel, gemmie, if I get fined ye'll jist get the caddle of yer ain eggs', meaning that to pay the fine he would just keep poaching to repay the fine. Geordie never heard anything further.

Some of the men kept snares, traps, ferrets and dogs for poaching and many a rabbit or hare has been left on our doorstep from an unknown caller.

My mother being Granny's only daughter left in the village meant that we had close ties. 'David, you had better go and see how your Granny is keeping.' Whether it was a couple of days or a week with my Granny, it was always, 'I hinna seen ye for a lang time – I'm needin errins' (messages). I got my instructions and a sixpence tied in a red and white spotted hankie. 'Noo, Davie, rin a yer feet an get a loaf, twa soft biscuits and a pennyworth o Jemisons fardens' (hard biscuits). There was me running like mad doon the lanes repeating, 'a loaf a loaf twa soft biscuits and a pennyworth of Jemisons fardens.' I would have been about seven then. 'Davie, keep the bawbee and dinna spen it a in ae shop' (changed days). One time my mother, along with some older cousins and I, took Granny into Aberdeen (I would have been ten at the time). Granny was out of her depth in all the Union Street traffic but, as hard as my relatives tried, they couldn't get her to go on a tram car, but when she took off her 'gaff topsail' (hat) on Union Bridge and started doing up her hair, they made a quick departure, leaving me holding the hat and hairpins. On one of my first trips to Aberdeen with my mother and deaf Isie (she wasn't so deaf then), and I would have been about five years old, they kept dragging me up and down Union Street, George Street, etc. I got lost in Woolworths and kept girning that my feet were sore and wanted down to the train to sit. Isie turned to me and said, 'Boyicky, if you dinna stop girning I'll chap ye.' I didn't get to the train but I did get to sit down in a café wi' a fine piece.

Mother was chatting to this woman one day and she remarked that she had heard that so and so was getting married to a Pole – Gena said, 'Maggie Ann, Poles, Poles, the quines nooadays wid merry claes poles if they hid breeks on.' This was related to my mother by another relative, who was asking Granny Mary about a bairn's name. Maggie to Granny: 'That's an awfa fancy name that Helenie his geen her bairn, fa's that ca'd efter.' Granny Mary – 'I'll seen tell ye fa that's ca'd efter, jist greed and ill manners.' The meaning of this was that the child was called after a distant wealthy relation in the hope of some inheritance later.

Granny was forever washing and demanded that my mother send our clothes across to her to be washed but she scrubbed them to bits in no time and was very annoyed when my mother got a hand-operated washing machine (they're just for the lazy folk). On Mother's washing day, I had to fill the boiler from the rainwater storage tank, light the fire and watch for Mr. Strachan (Non) to see what the weather was going to be like. He was a very good weather forecaster. He went through our close every day on the way to his daughters. After the clothes were washed and put through the mangle, they were taken down to the links where they were strung on clothes lines. On drying they were taken back to the house and ironed with the old fire heater method. You had two heater bricks, used one in the iron and, when it got cold, you took the other one out of the fire and put it in the iron. There was an ironing device which was heated by methylated spirits but it was erratic in behaviour and also rather smelly. After I installed the electrical system we were able to have an electric iron.

My parents also had what I believe was the first gramophone in the village. It had the winding-up handle and the large cone-shaped horn which was screwed into the mouth piece. The records were Harry Lauder, McCormack Dawson, Isabel Bailly, Caruso and also Messiah and Elijah. Our dogs used to sing, or rather howl, when they heard the gramophone; also, if you played the mouth organ in their presence, they joined in. I'm not sure whether it was disgust or pleasure. When my mother felt the shop was getting a bit too much for her, she sold out to a Mr. Gall, who also bought other properties in the village. He died in a home, a centenarian. Leeby Ann helped in the shop and later ran it for him. Mrs. Gall looked after the Post Office side but died before Mr. Gall. There was a burglary in the later stages of its existence. I cannot ever imagine that happening in our time. The stores were often unlocked as the dogs were real watchdogs, better than locks and keys.

In Loving Memory of Provost Peter Buchan
who was killed on the 18th October 1938 aged 59 years

No doubt such an unexpected sudden call
Will be remembered by one and all
We never know how near's the end
When we leave home, like our dear friend.

Such a useful man has been called away
Who served his town from day to day
To join a higher service than on earth
Where there are no partings, tears nor death.

Loved and respected far and near
At the funeral service flowed many a tear
All feelings went out for the two loved ones
As a cloud had shadowed their dear homes.

But there's a better day coming on
When we shall meet all loved ones gone
And join together in the sweet by and by
In that beautiful land beyond the sky.

The world has nothing lasting for you or me
It's just like a stormy troubled sea
Rich and poor have their ups and downs
As partings and trials o'er all abound

'Tis sweet to know as we travel on
No tears to dim the eye in our Father's home
When the two loved ones shall rise again
For ever with their Lord to reign.

Just in the hour that we think not
How often it comes to be our lot
Just like our brother and infant's case
Life is as a shadow, a very short race.

'Be ye also ready' is the call to all
As we never can tell what may befall
But although parted from our sight
We will cherish them in memory bright.

John Innes – Fisherman – Portnockie

Mr. Innes was known as the Fisherman poet, he had several copies of the above poem printed and distributed widely. The provost title is perhaps an overstatement but there were some people who addressed him as such. He left school early and was more or less self educated and he studied the Bible a lot and leaned towards the fundamentalist understanding of the Bible. He was a member of the Congregationist church for many years, also the Christian Endeavour, but during the diversion in this church, he left and was engaged in religious activities in most organisations. He then started a small mission in the village which was not attached to any church and he got speakers from all denominations, also freelance speakers: Salvation Army – People's

Mission, Deep Sea Mission, Church Ministers, Gordon Mission, Open Brethren, Faith Mission. Most of the speakers stayed in our house. He would never sit down to a meal without saying grace. Money didn't mean a great deal to him. I remember once he discovered that Quarriers' Homes wanted a car and he drove his own down South and donated it to the home.

Buchans

Far did a the Buchans come fae
And tae hae landed in this ae spot
Some say there wis twa lots
And some say twa's ower muckle
Some say they came frae Norway
An ithers fae nearer home
But farever they did come fae
There's ower muckle in St. Combs

The Buchan clan they span the world
Of that there is no doubt
You'll find them in Australia
Or fighting for the States
There's lots of them in Canada
The Blue Toon and the Broch
Be they upside doon or right way up
Their forebears man come fae Buchan

My father was named Patty
My mither was Maggie Ann
Their himist name was Buchan
And I'm anither o' the clan
There's Lords and lairds named Buchan
And Buchans that selt milk
There were Buchans that were diplomats
But maist were hameower folk

And when you come to Buchan
Pop down and see St. Combs
It has miles of open spaces
And bonny golden sands

There are nae regulations
And they dinna charge tae park
There's naebody tae harass ye
And I'm sure that you'd come back.

There is now a Hotel on the brae near the Brick Wall and Tillyduff, the Tufted Duck. It sells drink. Guid kens whit the auld folkies wid think. They've biggit the place where they used to bark the nets and where we bairnies used to play golf and drive across the brick wall stripe to a holie on the auld fitba pitch beside the Tillyduff. There was a rumour for a time that there was to be a golf course right across to the 'gallas' and back on a lower level to the Cample and the Brick Wall. There was also a rumour that a well-known professional had a look round and declared it suitable, but unfortunately nothing came of the proposal. Cruden Bay was chosen.

Another thing my father spoke about was the possibility of exploiting the old canal. I am sure there are a lot less favourable places which have been used. The Loch of Strathbeg is now being used as a bird reserve and all the way from Raltray Head to St. Combs would be suitable for a holiday camp or some other leisure activity.

The Mission Hall

When my father bocht a car,
He biggit a garage tae put it in
But seen he turned that muckle garage
Inta a mair up market use
He made it inta a little Kirkie
As their wis nae kirk in oor village
And then he got some planks and boxes
To seat the folkies that wid come
Then later on he got a joiner
To mak some mair better benches
A lot of folkies came to that garage
To sing the Sankey and Redemption songs
The Psalms and Paraphrases
The folkies were sae weel shuited
They put a sign up on the garage
And named that garage 'Bethel'
He wis reel read on Bible matters
And had a lot of books about it

He preached himself and invited ithers
To Sabbath services at eleven and three
He held meetings for the bairnies
And these services were often packed
And seen that garage got ower sma'
For a' that socht tae come and worship.
At that time some local joiners
Were signing on the dole in Broch
Wi' the help of these dole joiners
Anither Bethel it was built
At the bottom end o' Church Street.
This new Bethel was fitted oot
Wi' seats and fleer and a richt pulpit.
The preachers came fae far and near
To help oot with the services
But a' that came to a sudden end
When Dad was killed in a motor smash
The Bethel it wis never the same
Without his han tae guide it
The Salvation Army took it ower
But didna hae the same success
And sadly for the village folkies
The Bethel it wis burned doon
And noo a hoose his been biggit on't
Upon the Bethel found – The Church's Foundation.

The Gallows Steen

Oh fit stories that steen could tell ye
It man hae been there since time began
The Strandloupers must hae been there first
And hung a' them that blocked their path.
The Buchan folk came on the scene
They killed and skinned baith man and beast
And clad themselves in fur and hide
They thieved and plundered a' ower the place
And some were hung upon that rock
Were left there hingen till they rotted
Or were eaten up by birds and beasts
And when those Danes attacked oor shores

Them that quidna rin sae fast
Were teen and hung upon that steen
And if you dig aroon that rock
Yer sure tae fin a hantle o' beens
But fa's they are wid be hard tae ken
A Dane, a murderer, or a thief,
But noo they hae a common grave
Though maybe nae six fit o'earth
So when ye ging ower the Strype
And walk along the Keppickenslack
Then hae a lookit at that steen
And pit yer luggie tae its side
And maybe you will hear its story
Like you hear the sea fae a buckie shallie.

Village Tales and Sayings

Jecky and Muff were sitting on the braes and discussing who had the best eyesight:

Muff – 'Jecky, can ye see that midgie taken ower the tap o Mormond?'

Jecky – 'See that midgie, I just saw him winking tae his neeper.'

Jecky sent his son down to Billy Organ (Strachan) to get a hen to sit on eggs.

Boy – 'My fadder's sicen a clocken hen (broody) tae sit on eggs.'

Billy – 'A clocken hen to sit on eggs, boy, I'll gie ye a clocken hen that will sit on redd steens' (riding stones: these stones were used to anchor the yawls when fishing.)

Putler was a local character. He used to purchase an old boat for a few pounds and beach it on the St. Combs shore. He and his sons used to break it up with sledge hammers, wedges and cross-cut saws. The wood was mostly pitch pine and was taken up to their yard by cart and horse (Suzie). Suzie was also used on their country fish round. They had an old motor-driven circular saw that they cut up the boat timbers and decking. The blocks were then chopped up for firewood. As young lads we used to enjoy chopping up the blocks. The firewood was then sold round the village with Suzie and cart.

A visitor to my house asked me what I wanted to be when I grew up and I replied that I would like to be like auld Putler and chap sticks. Several of the village lads used to gather round Putler and listen to his words of wisdom as we chopped sticks. He said we didn't appreciate how lucky we were as regards education because he left school at twelve to go to sea. He asked some of us to speak the foreign language they had been learning. My older brother had started French so he said, 'Put a la motrie et Suzie', meaning, 'Put [Putler] has a motor and Suzie.' Put was quite impressed.

101

This worthy was walking from St. Combs to Peterhead (fourteen miles) and had got rather tipsy on the way, falling asleep at the roadside. Everytime he woke up and asked anyone where they were going it was always to St. Fergus. Sandy – 'Bless my soul, a' the wardle must be in St. Fergus.'

This young lad was courting a girl in the next village and he usually walked along the sands. He always tied a piece of cloth round his leg on the seaside in case a fog came down, and when he turned round and came back he changed the cloth to the other leg on the way back.

This gentleman had a rather large family of girls, but at last a boy was produced. I asked him how the new arrival was doing. 'David, he is doing fine but he's like an odd vase in a "ragmans cairt" [costermonger's barrow] – odd one out.'

This same man was asked how he had such a large family: 'Oh, I'm just obeying my minister's instructions, his text was to "multiply and replenish".'

Wullie kept coming into the shop for a bottle of Aspirin every other day. I asked him what he was doing with all the aspirins and he replied, 'Oh, I jist throw them awa.' Me – 'What do you buy them for?' Wullie – 'Oh, I have awfa sair lugs and I need the cotton waddin oot o the bottle tae pit into my lugs wi some olive oil.'

A visitor to the village was rather proud of his Doric. He met Robbie hobbling along with a stick. 'Well, Robbie, fit ails ye?' Robbie – 'Well, its like this, I wis awa poachen and I lowpit a stunk and straint mi queets. They're getting a bittie youkie noo. Wis ever ye fashed wi youkie queets.' It wouldn't sound the same when translated.

Mary and Charlie had gone to Aberdeen for the day and had got separated, they being on either side of Union Street. Charlie spotted Mary at Market Street and shouted across to her, 'Just bide there, Mary, I'll be across at the next sma' (lull in traffic).

Onack's Andy was a batchelor and was watching the high school girls enjoying themselves during their break – 'Now, girls, you enjoy life to the full, this is the best time of your lives.' 'What about our courting and loving days, Sir?' Andy – 'Well, I don't know about them, but there are a lot of women not happy with their men.'

This young lad was quite a character and sometimes became rather obstreperous. On this occasion he got beyond his father's control and he sent for the boy's Uncle who was rather strict. Wulzie gave the lad a real going over about being a disgrace to his parents, etc., etc. This went on for some time until the lad could take no more and, turning to his uncle, he said, 'Have you finished now, Uncle William? If not, it's high time you had for you are far too clever for this present evil world, you should have been living in the times of Abraham or Moses when they were bringing water from rocks and splitting seas in half – so run away home, Uncle, for even a worm will turn.'

This same lad had one of the earliest motor cycles in the village and was always careering about in a wild manner. He stopped to pick up Jeemsie and charge along the road, Jeemsie with his eyes shut. Jeemsie said, 'Hiv we far to go now, Bill?' 'Well, Jeemsie, you have just passed Annie Crookie and she's never very far from home.'

Andra was on his usual walk when he met the minister.

Andra – 'It's funny I should meet you. I wis dreamin last night aboot Heaven. I was going up to the golden stairway when I met St. Peter, who gave me a piece of chalk and said to write all my sins on the board provided.'

Minister – 'And was I there Andra?'

Andra – 'Aye, ye certainly were.'

Minister – 'And what was I doing?'

Andra – 'You were coming down the stairs for anither bit o chalk.'

These two men were in conversation when this good-looking spinster passed. 'What dae ye think o her?'

'A nae sae bad, but I think she's got tickets on hersel.' (Meaning that she fancied herself).

'Maybe she would make a good second wife, Bob.'

Bob – 'Well, John, maybe a man should hae a second wife looked oot but I have my one in the hoose and I'm nae looking for a third.'

This batchelor always used to sit and watch the boats passing and us lads used to encourage him to reminisce, as we knew what he would say. 'Aye, Jim that's a richt big steamer.'

Jim – 'Bye the day, bye the day noo man, a rasher o ham and twa fried eggs bye the day, man, home to the pretty girls bye the day noo, man.'

Our household was very fond of animals and we had cats, dogs, ponies, pigeons, bantams, rabbits, tortoises, hedgehogs, goldfish – you name it, we had it. Many brought their injured animals along. I had a wild duck swimming in our tank and after recovering it stayed with the bantams for a while. We had a bantam cock, which if allowed out, would chase the kids, pecking at their heels. We also had a little bantam who never grew up and we called him 'wee peep' and kept him in a little basket on the large range in the kitchen. He eventually died – the other bantams did not take to him. The two dogs we had during my younger days were Jock and Tibby. Jock was a curly Scottish retriever and Tibby was a wire-haired fox terrier. Betty, our pony, had hurt her leg and the vet was expected. The vet went straight to the stable but Jock and Tibby were lying beside the pony and wouldn't let him in. I had to go with him before the dogs would let him touch the pony. A further story about Jock and Tibby – Wellum (Bumble's William), who spent a lot of time around our house and buildings, was very ill and his father asked him if there was anything he wanted. 'Aye, I would like to see Patty's dog and pony.' He died a few days after this and Jock, the first time he got off the chain, went straight to William's house. His father came down to the shop and asked someone to come up as Jock was at the window with his front paws on the sill and he wouldn't move. When the service was held and the coffin being carried out, Jock started the most terrible howling and my mother had to go and settle him as we were all at the service. The houses were about 200 yards apart.

My pal Peter and I were down at the beach baiting our shore line when this lad came along and started to pull our line up. I asked him to stop but he paid no attention. Jock put his paws on his chest and gripped his arm. I said, 'Now you'll put the line back as it was,' which he did and we had no further trouble. Jock and Tibby were also in great demand as ratters. I used to take them along the beach when the tide was out (especially at night). Frisky, the cat, used to come along as well, rollicking with the dogs. At night when the tide was back the rats used to go and scavenge between the low and high tide water marks. Many a rat has come to grief in this way at the hands, or rather mouths, of Jock and Tibby.

Some fishermen used to bark (cure) their nets on the links and after drying would stack them up for transport. Rats used to shelter under them and Jock and Tibby were in attendance to knock them off when the nets were lifted. Also at threshing time on the local farms as the last few sheafs were being lifted, the rats would scamper out to be snapped up by the dogs. Other stables and premises would sometimes shelter rats and the dogs often got the call to do the needful.

We had the first crystal set in the 2.LO days and we had many visitors to hear the new invention. The first wireless we used had glowing valves (bright emitters). The sets were powered by wet batteries (accumulator) for LT (low tension) two volts and for the High Tension HT – normally 120 volts. Many came to wear the earphones and, even when the set went into oscillation, they thought it was high class music. There were some that would have nothing to do with the infernal machine, as they thought it could pick up other household conversations.

Later, I used to go round the village and do the odd repair and also sell a few wireless sets which I built at home; later still, the complete set could be obtained from wholesalers.

The Mannie

Ye ken this kind of mannie weel
He wis never verra guid at skweel
And hidna sae muckle up on tap
But man he kent a shillens worth
He bocht an auld boatie awfa chep
And beached her on a Spring high tide
He chappit her up for kenlin sticks
Then selt the sticks aroon the toon.

Wi the siller he launched oot
He bocht a chop in anither toon
Selt athing there from preens tae ploos
And wis weel kent for his fair dealing
Anither chop he seen bocht
And seen it wiz half a dizzen
He then gid in for selling cars
They came to him from near and far.

He bocht a fermie nae far fae toon
Wi hens and coos and haflin loons
And they did weel for simple him
He must have had the midas touch
For aa he did jist seemed tae fluer
He gid weel tae needy causes
Nae tae buy a place up there
But as a gift for his guid fortune.

Some hae brains and nae much cash
But seem quite happy wi their lot
And that my freens' fit matters maest
Siller and gowd they may glitter
But sometimes can be a bittie slippy
Ging throwe yer hands like saft soft
Ae day yer up on the riggen tile
The neist yer doon right on yer dowp.

The Drain

Anint the Pot and Sanny Banks
There wis an affa affa drainie
It gid aff an affa stink
Especially fin it wis haet.
If there wis nae a sole aboot
And if it wis, jist affa quaet
The rottens, gulls and craws did gether
Tae see fit they quid get tae ait.
The drain it came fae the killin hoose
Jist ower the brae a bittie.
And as we bairnies played nearby
We often hid tae cross that stink
We held oor breath and grippt oor nose
And ran ower it that bittie sharpish
We thocht that affa affa stink
Wid gie us a the fivver
But noo that drainie his dried up
Nae coos bleed noo tae mak a stink
The killen hoose is sae quaet
Nae noises noo fae pigs or coos
Its bye the day, its bye the day.
But I mine fine the time that we
Gid doon there tae get a blidder
And blaw it up for us tae kick
When we quidna get a fitba.
I mine tee fin that killen hoose
Wis a gey bit steeren placie
The coos were kilt and cut in half
And wrappit up in clean hessian
Then taken tae the station siden
Pit in a wagon wi special insulation
The trainie picket up that wagon
And awa it went tae London toon
Tae Smithfield market or ither place
And in the chops it was selt
As the best – Prime Scottish beef.
Nae killen hoose, nae butchers chop
It's jist like maest ither things

Its super this and super that
In fact its jist aboot super athing
The local shoppies they're jist super
For odds and ends and things like papers.

My Dream

I hid a dream the ither nicht
It took me back in time
To when I wis a wee bit loon
Aye fleein aboot oor ain wee toon
Mi doggies were there beside me
Aye looken up at me
Tae see if there wis a piecie
Or a sweetie fae the chop.
And there wis Jimmy Officer
Wi his mullie o' brown snuff
Pitten a drappie on his neive
And snuffen it up his nose.
A bittie further up the road
There wis this boorichie of men
Catta, Mull and Sammy Put
Newsen tae their hairts content
And sooken at their cutty pipes
The rick it gid ower their heads
Like a thrashen mull at 'Widdies'
And in that awfa rick I'm sure
There were mair spunks than boggie
At that time there wis nae wurd
O smoken and its dangers
To them it wis jist een
O their verra few enjoyments,
As I went doon the brae
There wis Nonter wi his cheese cutter
On his wye tae dig for lug.
And then I heard the trainee fussle
Tae tell the folkies it wis comen in
And that they must jist hurry up
If they did want to catch it.
There wis Polly's Isie Ann

And Billy Organ's Gena
Hurrying down past Onack's hoose
Wi their baskets and their creelies
Tae catch the trainie for the Broch
An tae sell their fish roon Strichen toon.
There wis Dody Fitie's Jeanicky
And Bessie Jack her sister
Wi their creels and baskets
Makken for the trainie tee
To sell their fish tae ferms and crafts
Aroon Auchnagatt or Brucklay
And there wis cripple Annie
Nae makken for the train
But up the road tae crafts and ferms
Roon aboot Savoch and Millhill.
Noo before I gid hame again
I went to see mi granny
There she wis in the washen hoose
Wi tub and soapy suds
Scrubbing on the boordie
Tae get her washen fite.
As I gid hame I met up
Wi Katie's Jeck and famely
Pitten his bikie a the gither
Tae get him tae the Broch
And as he tried tae start it
Wi the kick start and a run
It gave a mighty backfire bang
That woke me fae mi dream.
And that wis jist as weel
For the chumly knock said seven
I hid tae rush mi brakfist
But caught the train tae Broch
Mi ain wee knockie it hid stoppit
I'd forgotten tae win it up
And if you dream of times lang past
Be sure ye win yer knockie up.

There was a family in the village which was very unfortunate. Most of the family were mentally weak, some of them never got out at all. A sister and a brother were well known in the village, the sister was able to go for messages but the boy went around the village swinging a rope above his head, lengthening and shortening it all the time, but they were quite harmless. Both parents were normal, the father especially was very well read and particularly regarding the Bible.

A lot of the villagers were beachcombers, going along the beach to pick up any flotsam or jetsam which may have been thrown up there. During the wars lots of booty was picked up, especially when a cargo boat had been torpedoed. As boys we used to sing a ditty, where it came from I don't know. More than likely it had been handed down from our parents. It ran as follows:

> There was a gallant steamer
> *The Union* was her name
> She struck the rocks near Rattray
> And her cargo was scattered wide.
> As Topsen's Robsie came over the san
> He got a cloot washen in wi a run
> He picked it up and he carried it home
> But he got it teen fae im
> By long boatman Tom.

Davie West was a cousin of mine and he tells this story about the time he spent as a house doctor in Aberdeen Infirmary. He was showing this Professor round the ward when he came to this St. Combs patient. Davie: 'This is Miss Cow, she has a suspected stomach ulcer and is being kept under observation.' He got no further.
Patient – 'Davie, Westie, dinna Miss Cow me, abody kens me as Deerick's Titt and it's me stamick that's wrang. Aa I need is guid mulk maet.'

Another one Davie tells, he was doing the rounds with this surgeon when he came to this patient. Surgeon – 'Weel, Annie, fit like the day?' Annie – 'Nae sae bad, Doctor, but fit ails me?' Surgeon – 'Weel, Annie, it's jist like this, yer gettin on in years and yer in-timmers are gyan deen but there's a lot o life in ye yet, my dear.'

Jocky was on a return visit to the village after spending some time away. His sister was at the station to meet him and found he was talking rather posh. She left him with another relative and ran down to her mother with the following. Sally – 'Midder, Jockie's come, he's ca'in a steen a stone, a been a bone and a cat a long-tailed animal and he says to me I'm blowed if I know you, Sally.'

Another in the same vein: this girl had been teaching in England and on her way home discovered her small brother playing in a pool of water in the street. Girl – 'Billy, will you please come out of that duck's puddle and not file yer breeks.' Father – 'Noo, Bella, just behave yersel, yer hame noo, just speak like ither folk for yer gyan all down throwe it.'

Andrew Buchan (Daisy) was a neighbour of ours. He was awarded a D.S.C. for his actions during the Dunkirk evacuation. He took his drifter up to the beaches and ran up and down the beach shouting, 'Onybody fae Peterhead or The Broch this wye.' I was speaking to him about this after the war and told him that I had a D.S.C. before him. 'What did you get it for?' he asked. 'I got it for being born D.S.C.' (these being my initials).

Several of us young lads had been across to the Loch of Strathbeg on an egg collecting expedition and were on our way home when we were given chase by Mr. McIntyre and his son Johnny. We had several varieties of eggs for our collections. We were nearing the canal when William decided to take the eggs and plunge across the canal, which he did, and this allowed the rest of us to escape. William joined us later further along the links with a grin on his face. The canal was formed when a Mr. Seller decided to drain the Loch of Strathbeg in the early part of the nineteenth century but gave up due to the lack of cash and the drifting sands. The local women were seldom seen without their wiven (knitting), especially when waiting for their boaties to come in. This couple were sitting at the Cample wiven awa and discussing the quality of their worsit (wool). Mary – 'Is at oo?' Jessie – 'Aye, it's oo.' Mary – 'A' oo.' Jessie – 'Aye a' oo'.

I got many pairs of home-knitted socks and jerseys for favours I had carried out, they were a kindly and generous lot on the whole. The Second World War changed the village, there are now many strange names and the characters have disappeared to a large extent. I was using home-knitted socks for years after I left the village and my mother gave some away to visiting relatives.

There were very few Brethren in St. Combs, they were mostly church people. One of the Close Brethren had committed an indiscretion and was up in court. The Magistrate was about to pass sentence when he was interrupted by the accused. 'Excuse me, sir, I wish to plead not guilty, it was the flesh that committed the crime.' Judge – 'In that case, I condemn the flesh to six weeks in jail.'

Sandy Buchan (Save), who was a school mate of mine, told me this story: he went into Lizicky's shoppie for a joiners pencil. 'I hinna ony joiners pencils, Sandy, will a pennyworth o' sweetie bools di instead?'

Charlie Lizzicky's brother used to come down and borrow our barrow to sell ice-cream. He used to trundle the barrow and freezer round the village shouting, 'Ony bairns, Ony bairns – Ice-Cream.'
As kids we used to sing this ditty about Charlie:

> 'Ice-cream done wafers too
> What is Charlie going to do
> But hurl the barrow back home.'

I was staying in a house for a short time and there were a couple of teachers there as well. One morning, one of the teachers, whilst we were having breakfast, remarked that she had a terribly restless night dreaming about cows. The other teacher turned to Wullie (grandson). 'And did you dream about cows as well, William?'
Wullie – 'Dinna be feel, I wisna sleepin' in the same bed.'
Another time Wullie was given a sixpence by one of the teachers for going a message. Wullie went out spent his sixpence on a bag of softies. The teacher, expecting him to buy sweets, said, 'Why did you buy softies?' Wullie – 'Well I heard Granny speaking about hard times and I thocht that would keep her going for a wee while.'
This young boy was at a kid's party and was eating away at the goodies when the hostess said, 'Well, Doddy, have you had enough to eat?' Doddy said, 'Weel, wifie, I'm full but I'm nae stappit' (packed).
Davie and I were out on a trip this very warm day and called into a hole-in-the-wa shoppie and asked for two lemonades. She poured my one into a glass and went into the rear of the shop, emptied her false teeth out of the glass and, without cleaning, served Davie's lemonade in it. I couldn't let him know as the daughter was standing close by. I never did tell him as I am sure he would have been sick. What had been in my own glass before!
A grandfather of one of the village lads had discovered that his grandson had won some money gambling at cards. He was very angry about this and went to the card school and threw down the money on the ground, declaring, 'One and tipence or thripence, I'm nae sure which, but its oor Dodie's boy's bawbees and I'm for nae ill gotten gains in my hoose. Guid day tae ye.'
Rosie Jean used to go round the village houses with her basket exchanging roses (artificial) for rags or other odds and ends. Matheson was the ragman and with his cairt collected rags and rabbit skins in exchange for a bowl or plate. There were Ingen Johnnies, Silka Blouse, an Indian gentlemen selling clothes; Mr. Woolfe, a Jew, selling furs, and several tinker

families who camped on the links. Some used to visit the shop: 'A penny packet o' tea, Mr., and can you give some old cheese and old biscuits for the bairns?' One pair we used to call 'Murder' as they were always fighting when they had a little too much to drink, the wifie shouting murder at the top of her voice. But the tinkers left so much rubbish behind them that they were stopped from camping.

This story I was involved in when one stifling summer day a thunder and lightning storm arose and our shop and house were hit. Lizzie Strachan was sitting on the stool in the telephone room when the strike occurred: there was a terrific bang and Lizzie was knocked off the chair and the phone went dead. I was in the kitchen and was rather scared and was passing the kitchen range when I felt a warm air and was knocked to the ground. Picking myself up off the floor, I ran through the connecting door to the shop where there was a great commotion. Several people came running in as they said they saw this ball of fire strike the telephone pole at the rear of the shop. There were no casualties apart from the phone being out of order. The telephone earthing system had done its work. For a long time afterwards, I was really scared when there was a lightning storm. After joining the telephone service, I got over it and became quite familiar with the damage caused by lightning.

There was no tailor in St. Combs, so you had to walk to Tailor Geddes (Park, Lonmay) or to Tailor Shaw (Bruxie Rathen). Wullie required a new suit and was preparing for his hike to the tailor. His wife's instructions were as follows – 'Noo, Wullie, tak this leg o rabbit in yer pooch and a piece, gin stracht there an stracht back and nae half-wye houses and nae newsin on the wye and be back before dark.'

There were certain houses where the men used to meet and put the world to rights, play dambrods (draughts) or dominoes. Such houses were Johnny Grevie's, Muff's, Officer's, Daisy's, to name but a few. Many stories originated at these houses or at the rudder. The rudder was behind the old cemetery wall, an old boat's rudder was used to stand on. Johnny Grevie was a batchelor and they used to tease him about a certain woman. Says Johnny, 'I had somebody looked out but she had a "ringel-e"' (wall-eyed).

A Salvation Army lassie was collecting in the village and asked Dave for a donation. Dave – 'Foo auld may ye be, lassie?' Lassie – 'Oh, I'm just twenty.' Dave – 'Well I'm ower eighty so I hid better give my donation personally as I'm likely to see him before you.' The lassie got her donation as well.

Alick Duncan had been pestering his father for football boots to no avail. One day whilst shaving his father, he had shaved half the father's face when he said, 'What about football boots?' and the answer was still in the negative. Alick said, 'Well in that case you had better get Nan to shave the other half, I'm awa tae the fitba.'

This story relates to one of the local doctors who had been attending. Charlie, one of the local farmers. He advised him to give up the bottle right away or reap the consequences, but Charlie said that surely that would be too big a change and be a shock to his system. 'Well, Charlie, not any more than one ounze a day.' After the Doctor had gone, Charlie said to his maid, 'Come on now, Jean, give me my ration.' Jean – 'You heard fit the doctor said, jist one ounze a day, but Maester, foo am I tae ken fit one ounze is?' 'Well, Jean, ye wis at skweel the same as me and fit dis it say, sixteen drams equals one ounze.'

These are two other doctor stories. The first was a reply to a maternity claim: 'In answer to your letter, I have given birth to a little boy weighing 10 lbs., is this satisfactory?'

The second was a sickness claim: 'I want my money as quickly as possible as I have been in bed with the doctor for a week and he doesn't seem to be doing me any good.'

As I have mentioned before, my cousin Davie was a doctor. He's a good bit older than me and once took me into one of his lecture rooms where there was a skeleton in a glass class. 'See that mannie in the gless case?' he said, 'fin ever he hears twelve o'clock ring at night he's oot o that case like a shot.' I couldn't get out quick enough. I had a few lookie roons on my way out to see he was still in his case, even although it wisna twal at nicht.

This woman did not approve of her daughter's latest suitor and addressed him at her door as follows: 'I'm nae for nae cursen, I'm nae for nae swearin. Oor Mary Bella jist nae gyan and yer nae gyan tae be hingin yer bonnet in my hoose for I'm nae gyan to be the "stocken laff" o' onybody, guid day tae ye, man. Dinna darken my door again.' Spoonerism – stocken laff (laughing stock).

Sweemology

As I sat on the Kirky Brae
Wi a my couthie cronnies
Listening to their claik and banter
Tae a their guid times and mishanters,
Then Jeemsie said, 'Noo, Davie lad,
Jist listen to my story

Aboot the twa young fisher loons
And this oh so learned chielly.
They went to sea one day to fish
Wi hanlins and wi rippers
But this oh sae clever mannie
Kept on about their failings.
A third of life they had missed
They'd never studied Psychology
Anither third gid doon the drain
This time it was geology
But just then a lump o' sea
It cowpit up the yawlie
The three of them were in the sea
All strugglin for survival
When Robbie cried, 'Professor Sir,
Do you know about Sweemology?
If not, my man, then I'm afraid
Your whole life is in jeopardy.'

The Worthy

He sits there on the Kirky Brae
His doggie by his side
A dreaming and a yearning
For the days of auld lang syne
When he left his mither's hoosie
Some foreign pairts to see,
A spy glass and a compass
His relics of the sea

As he sits there on the braeside
And gazes out to sea
A passing steamers siren blows
And jolts him back in time
Then picking up his spy glass
He brings her into view
And mutters to himself, alas
How different it could be.

He sits there on the braeside
Still looking through his glass
His mind it starts to wander
To that dim and distant past
When he left his mither's hoosie
An his bonny lassie Jean
She chose anither strappin chiel
And he was on his lean

Still sitting on the braeside
His doggie at his feet
Anither cronnie comes along
And Sandy he did gibe
Aye, Sandy man, it's Jean again
I can tell it by yer een
Her man's been deed a filey noo
And Jean came hame the streen

Aye, Jecky man, fits that ye say
That Jean, came back the streen
Her mither's hoosie tae redd out
That's music tae ma ears
Noo, Jecky man, I must awa
And get a bite o' maet
An gie my face a bittie dicht
Afore I call on Jean.

Noo Sandy and his doggie Mac
Set oot to call on Jean
Outside the door were cleaning things
A pail, a brush, a cloot
And on the door he chappit loud
And Mac and he did wait
And in a tic there was Jean
Aye-richt before his een.

Her blushing made her bonny
Nae doubt about her kennan
'Come ben the hoose – It's Sandy, Mam,
The kettles on the bile.'

The Hoosie wis jist spick and span
And Jean she wis a topper
They news'd and news'd for half the nicht
As if they'd never pairted.

Now Sandy, Mac and Jean as well
Are in her mither's hoosie
And Jecky, Tam and Davie tee
They are his faithful callers
His gairden and his ither jobs
His Jean has made a pleasure
The Kirky Brae sees less o' him
As does his former treasures.

Funny Speaking

A lang time seen
I gid down Sooth
Tae see a fitba' match
I went to see some folkies
That came fae oor hame toon
They made me mair than welcome
Wi breed and cheese and ham
There were lots of fancy pieces
An sweeties aye at·han
We talked and talked and nattered on
Aboot Patty, Muff and Non.
Their little laddie stood there
And nae a word he kent
He said to me, 'Why David, You do talk so very funny.'
I said to him, 'Noo, laddie, just you wait
Til' you come north to Scotland
To see yer Dide and Granny
It will be you not me
That will talk and talk sae funny.'

The Germans

I heard this tale fae word o' mou'
It's truth I canna vouch for

About this twa young fisher loonies
That came fae oor hame toonie
Who went to fecht the Kaiser
But got trappit wi' the Hun
They spent some time in cages
And were questioned by the Bosch
Wi' maps and buiks and pencils
They tried to pin them doon
But the funny way these laddies spoke
Had the Germans sae dum foonert
That they let the loonies oot o' jyle
Tae wander far and wide.
They landed up North in Russia
Jist lumps o' skin and been
And caught a boat tae Scotland
That landed them in Leith
And then they got anither
That took them tae the Broch.
Noo these twa fisher laddies
Lived lang and weel content
Wi' fisher laddies o' their ain
And bonny quinies as weel
And all because the way they talked
Wis jist that bittie funny.

Inverallochy and Cairnbulg are only a couple or so miles across the links from St. Combs and yet the accent and some of the words are different. For example, in St. Combs the word **hold** would be **had**, whilst across the way it would be **hod**. **Sand** would be **san** and **soan – stand** would be **stan and stone**. In St. Combs, crab traps are known as trunks (troonks) not as creels. A seagull in St. Combs is a meave, not a scurry. A large tern was called mossick or moss tarrick. A coot was a bullqueet. A mast is a most. Pirries were small fish known as baddocks in some places and these we caught from the rocks with a line and black theukies (hookies); when fish reached nine inches or thereabout they were known as poddlies, then around twelve inches saithe. Conger eels were known as haevels, these were used for troonk bait along with other fish such as dog and cat fish.

A plaice was a plash, a freshick was a freshwater or flounder, these we caught on our shore lines until the trawling baldies cleaned up the shories.

Crab names were partans, labsters, peels, pillers, reedicks, greenicks, bushicks and safticks. Crabs (craibs) – Partans, labsters (lobsters), peels and pullers have been touched on already; reedicks were reddish coloured craibs not suitable for bait, a greenick was a greenish craib also not suitable for bait. A bushick was a female crab with eggs attached. A saftick was the soft crab after it had cast its shell, suitable for bait if not too hard. Male and female crabs were distinguished by what we called their purse, the folding portion on the crab's belly. The male crab had a much narrower purse than the female.

When the Inverallochy golf course was in use there was one particular occasion which deserves mention and this was when a delegation of golfing M.P.s played the local club and the local golfers were the victors. Anecky's Jeek was one of the local stalwarts. Since its revival, the club has produced some good golfers.

Twa Buchan sodgers were in this French toonie when they saw this large wedding taking place and they tried to find out who the dignitaries were. All they could pick up was that someone named Jean Nissie Pah was involved. Ten days later they saw this large funeral and again tried to find out who was dead and discovered it was Jean Nissie Pah. Goovie Dick's Sandy: 'He didna last lang, his wadden must hiv been ower muckle for him.'

Life

I wisna very guid at skweel
Wi' beuks or sums or spellin
I dinna think that I was thick
Though maybe a bittle glaiket
The teachers said I didna try
And maybe they were richt
But a' the lickens they gid me
Made not a whit of difference
Learnen wis for college chiels
And nae the likes o' me.

I left that awfa awfa skweel
Wi' nae sae muckle in mi heid
Wi' happy hert – tae pastures new.
I went to skweels and colleges
And held my own with most
My job it took me far and wide

To North and South to East and West
From Shetland to the Butt o' Lewis
And down the line to London town.
With over forty years of wandering
I thought I'd earned some time to rest.

And noo I've laid my Fordel bye
Its bools and golf and carries,
With rakes and spads thrown in between
Those leisure hours I'm spending noo
Wi' cronnies that are nae fae hame
But aye I tak a turnie doon
To see my old but changing toon
My hair its getting grey and thin
Jist like those couthie hamely folk
That I grew up wi' and did ken sae weel.

I have already quoted some of my granny's sayings and some I have heard around the village and in the shop. Here is a further list with a brief explanation. The first one is particularly pertinent to the village before it got its water supply.
'You never ken the want o'watter till the wall rins dry' – meaning, 'You'll never value water until there is none there.'
'An oor in the mornen is worth twa at night' – 'An hour in the morning is worth two at night.'
Feels and bairns shoudna see jobs half deen' – meaning, 'Fools and children should not see jobs half finished.'
'Ye need a lang speen tae sup wi' the deel' – meaning, 'Keep away as far as possible from trouble.'
'There's neen sae blin as canna see' – meaning, 'It's difficult for some to accept the obvious.'
'There's nae feel like an auld feel' – meaning, 'There is no fool like an old fool.'
'Auld age disna come its leen' – meaning, 'Old age brings its troubles.'
'Faur there's naething geen there's nothing required' – meaning, 'If there is nothing up top, nothing is expected.'
'Fin drinks in, wits oot' – meaning, 'Intoxication breeds stupidity.'
'Gweed aye helps them that help themsels' – meaning, 'The creator helps the industrious.'
'It's nae loss fit a freen gets' – meaning, 'It is no loss what a friend gets.'

'Keep yer ain fish guts tae yet ain sea-maas' – meaning, 'Look after your own – charity begins at home.'

'It's an ull win that blaws naebody gweed' – meaning, 'It's an ill wind that blows nobody good.'

'Pooder and pint hides mony a rent' – meaning, 'Don't be fooled by external appearances,' i.e. female adornment.

'The better the day the better the deed' – meaning, this is to justify working on a Sunday.

'The wullin' horse gets the maist work' – meaning, 'The willing horse gets most work.'

'The soutar's bairns are worst shood' or 'The tailor's bairns are worst claed' – meaning, 'the shoemaker's or tailor's children are always worst provided.'

'He's nae sae feel as his blate looken' – meaning, 'He is not so silly as he looks.'

'If the bonnet disna fit dinna weirt' – meaning, 'Don't take the blame if innocent.'

'A face like a torn scone', or

'A face like a coo's hin end', or,

'A face like a blunt aiz', or,

'A nib like the jib o' a cran,' or,

'A moo like a torn pooch,' or,

'A heid like hairy Mary' – meanings are all derogatory facial sayings.

'He's got a' his back teeth, yon een,' – meaning, 'He is no fool, pretty sharp.'

'It's a sair tyauve for a moufa o' maet' – meaning, 'A struggle for existence.'

'Man that fesses tae yer heart' – meaning, 'It does your heart good, a treat.'

'He's his ain worst enemy' – meaning, 'Misguided existence' – mostly drinkwise.

'She's bookelt like a circus horse' – meaning, 'Dressed to the nines.'

'Ony mair o' yer lip and I'll tak me han across yer face' – meaning, 'Any more impudence and I'll give you what for.'

'Mony hans mak licht work' – meaning, 'Many hands lighten the work.'

'Come on gies yer claik' – meaning, 'Come and give us your news.'

'The Peterheid girls – they're the boys' – meaning, 'The Peterhead girls are super.'

'The back o' me han tae ye, boy' – meaning, 'Not very good.'

'The day the coo calves' – meaning, 'A reward in prospects (pension), pay day.'

'Yer like the wifie's ae coo' – meaning, 'All together.'
'Yer like the coo's tail, aye ahin' – meaning, 'You're like the cow's tail, always behind.'
'There's a midst in a' seas' – meaning, 'There's a limit to all things.'
'As hard as Hennersin' – meaning, 'As hard as nails.'
'A the Jews are nae in Jerusalem' – meaning, 'All the Jews are not in Jerusalem, some are here' – the fly merchants.
'Come benn the hoose' – an entreaty with several meanings.
'Ae, yon een kens the richt side o' a shillin' – meaning, 'She knows the value – bargain wise.'
'Ye widna hae deen that tae him when he wis in his potestater' – meaning, 'You wouldn't have done that to him when he was at his peak.'
'Yon een wid miss an aal cloot fae the door' – meaning, 'She's pretty sharp and mean.'
'His bawbees are burnin' a hole in his pooch' – meaning, 'A child dying to spend his Saturday penny.'
'Back tae aal claes and porritch' – meaning, 'Back to the mundane duties.'
'It gings through his fingers like dirt,' – meaning, 'Careless with money.'
'It's nae a broken ship' – meaning, 'It's not a bottomless pit.'
'It a' comes oot o' the howell' – meaning, 'The fishing provides the where with all.'
'It's like sna' aff a dyke – Like water aff a dyeuks back' – meaning, 'Soon gone – it doesn't stick.'
'There's naethin' in his heid bit bawbees' – meaning, 'He's concerned only about money.'
'Mair hurry less speed' – meaning, 'False short cuts.'
'Yon een his a hoose like a byre (or midden)' – meaning, 'An untidy house' (dirty).
'The Dutch have invaded Holland' – meaning, a catchphrase for the unwary.
'Burnt bairns dreed the fire' – meaning, 'Burnt children are frightened of fire.'
'Like a hen on a haet girdle.' – meaning, 'Fidgety.'
'As scarce as the teeth o' hen,' – meaning, 'As nothing.'
This led to the often used wedding telegram: 'May yer joys be as thick as the sna in the glen and yer sorrows as scarce as the teeth o' a hen.'
'There's nithing in him but fit the speen pits in' – 'Little brain power.'
'Like a flea amon treakle' – meaning, 'In a mess.'
'Like a shooer o' skalte steens' – meaning, 'Pretty noisy.'

'He's aye at his midder's apron strings', or, 'He's his midder's bairn – a mam's loon' – meaning, 'A bit of a mother's boy.'

'Yer jist a Jeannie ottie' – meaning, 'Afraid of water' (sea bathing).

'Yer jist a dry dockey' – same as above.

'Yer jist a fearty' – meaning, 'You're just afraid.'

'He's a lang heid yon een' – meaning, 'He's no fool.'

'As peer as a kirk moose' – meaning, 'Pretty poor circumstances.'

This was displayed in a toilet:

> Keep it clean, ye muck vratches
> It's for yer urine nae yer matches.

'May the moose niver leave yer girnal wi' a tear in its ee' – meaning, 'May the mouse never leave the meal barrel with a tear in its eye.'

'Are yer lugs nae burnen?' meaning, 'We were just speaking about you.'

'A lang wye tae gin seen hame' – meaning, 'A roundabout way.'

'Ready and wallen like the lassies o' Cullen' – meaning, 'Ready and willing like the girls from Cullen.'

'I've seen the day, but noo it's nicht' – 'It's bye the day, it's bye the day' – 'It's bye twal o' clock noo' – meaning, 'The flush of youth is past.'

'Now over the hill.' 'Every doggie has its day.'

'A geen horse shidna be lookit in the mou' – meaning, 'A gift horse shouldn't be looked in the mouth.'

'Keep laich doon and ye hinna sae faur tae fa' – meaning, 'Keep a low profile and your fall won't be so great.'

'Fit thocht ye fin Jock socht ye? Wid ye hae im thocht ye?' – meaning, 'What did you think when Jock asked you? Would you have him?'

The Walk

Initially the walk was a temperance parade held every year, when every member of the band had to sign the temperance pledge and also to demonstrate his ability to play the flute, like playing 'Dare to be a Daniel'. The walk originated from the time of the cholera epidemic, periods of excessive drunkenness and a religious revival which ensued. After the revival drink was taboo, all public houses were closed and wages paid with booze stopped.

The three villages, Inverallochy, Cairnbulg and St. Combs each have their walks. Inverallochy walk is held on Christmas day, Cairnbulg on New Year's day and St. Combs on 'Auld Eel', but now on 2nd January. Each had their flute band which headed the parade, the male and female couples (in age of seniority) walked behind. The St. Combs parade assembled at the Kirky in High Street, had a tune up, then went down Charles Street to Charleston (Sodom), across the links to Inverallochy and Cairnbulg. The parade went round the two villages, followed by local relatives who gave the children fruit and sweets. They then returned to St. Combs via the links, going up Mid Street to the Kirky (Hall). Buses are now used.

Before the actual walk day, the band usually spent a week or so going round the countryside at night practising, visiting Manses, farms and big houses. One night we called on this minister and asked if we could play 'Onward Christian Soldiers'. 'No, no,' said he minister, 'that's for Sundays.' He asked, 'What about "Horsie, keep your tail up"?'

Pede (another Bruce) was in charge of the band on our night rehearsals, he was killed in one of the air raids on Fraserburgh.

On the walk itself the bellringer went round the village in the morning requesting all walkers to be at the Kirky by such and such a time. During the walk itself the tunes played were 'Dare to be a Daniel', 'Onward

123

Christian Soldiers', 'The Auld Hoos', 'Rowan Tree', 'Oh Come all ye Faithful', etc., etc. The same partners were seen together for several years. My partner was Jessie Bella (Cly's daughter). There was great rivalry between the various villages, such as who had the best and largest band and who had the most couples and who had the best concert and who had the most fur coats.

A lot of ex-St. Combers came from Fraserburgh and Peterhead, as well as some from further afield. The Peterhead contingent originally came in horse-drawn carriages (cabbies) hired for the day from Reid or Sutherland, but later buses were used. After arriving back at the Kirky, the couples dispersed to their various homes, to partake of the large meals. Nobody need go hungry on that day for there was an open door at most houses. In older times the meals were pretty ordinary but nowadays meals are varied and sumptuous, such as broth, beef, dumpling, steak pies, turkeys, hens, tinned fruit, jellies, trifles, with lashings of tatties and vegetables and plenty tea and coffee and fine pieces. After the inevitable gossip, it was another spread for tea before going to the concert (soirée). This was held in the Kirky and local talent was mostly used. The concert could be either sacred or secular depending on the decision of the walk committee. The sacred concert in earlier days may have been the 'Messiah', 'Elijah', 'David, the Shepherd Boy' and these may have been performed at other times as well. Sometimes the principals in the concerts would be known by the names they played: Magsie (Abigail), Cly (Saul), Paul Cruickshank (lum hat wanten a croon).

Our shop remained open during the walk day as the Post Office did not recognise it, so normal attendance was required, 8.00 a.m. to 7.00 p.m., so my parents did not have a walk dinner and I was always invited to my partner's house (Jessie Bella) for my walk dinner and to Inverallochy Post Office during the Inverallochy walk. As our shop was open on walk day, we always had customers for the forgotten items and maybe extras if the household had got more visitors than expected. Also for the concert there was a demand for sweets and cough lozenges. There was one item, 'sen sens' (liquorice sweets), which had an aromatic smell, scented the breath and soothed the throat, they were 2d. a packet and I haven't heard or seen them since.

If the weather was bad the train might be used to convey the walk to and from the villages. The last walk I attended was just after the war when my wife and I went down to my mother's. My wife went to the walk with my Uncle Clark while I went with his daughter Betty and a good day was had by all, with another two fur coats and broth and beef and dumplings.

The Walk

St. Combs was eence a dunken placey
The men vrocht hard for sma reward
And mony a man wis paid wi' drink
An mony a bairn had an empty belly.
A preacher man came tae the toon
He preached hell, fire and certain doom
Unless they stopped their evil ways
The upshot was the folkies turned
They closed the pubs and drink they spurned.
The result it was a temperance walk
To sign the pledge and demonstrate
So every year at New Year time
A band of flutes and drums parade
As village couples walk behind
Across the links to Bulgar toon
Then back again to eat their fill
A concert in the evening too
To further strengthen this resolve.
A' that it was, some time ago
The walk it is still on the go
But temperance now plays little part
A social function at the most
The concert then was sacred too
Not so now, its anything goes
The test tune then was strict and just
Twas 'Daniel Dare' the fluters must
But noo gweed kens, it's anything but.

The Broken Singer

Noo Bella was a bonny lass
And a bonny singer tee
She hid a voice just like a bell
And tae the concert she wis socht
Tae sing the sangs o' Robbie Burns.
Her midder wis o' sae shuited
And took her Bella tae Aberdein
Trailt up and doon a' ower the toon

Tae get a bonny silken goon
Noo come the nicht o' the concert
Her quine she was the best of a'
But as she sang her himist sang
She tripped up upon the wurds
And took her seat a broken lass.
Peer midder wis in sic a carfuffle
She took a dwaam and wis caerrit oot
We smellen salts they did revive her
But that was Bella's himist sang
An' noo she sits there in the audience
A broken 'belle' without a voice
Her bell like voice his been silent lang
Just like the bells that niver rang
Peer midder, Peer Bella, Peer concerts
And a jist ower aal Robbies sang
Noo fit wid Robbie say o' this
O that Gweed – A broken gift.

Deaths, Births and Marriages

When anyone died there was a long period of mourning. Most of the children in the village used to visit the house and be taken in to view the corpse, being uplifted by an assisting relative of the deceased. I remember once being lifted up to see this distant male relative and he had a penny on one eye, which greatly intrigued me. I discovered it was put there as seemingly one of his eyes hadn't closed. The local graveyard finally closed in the 1920s and the cemetery at Lonmay Church was used, but another cemetary near the Episcopalian Church was opened and my father and mother, their grandchild and granddaughter are buried there.

I remember one of the last funerals to take place in the old St. Comb's graveyard was Johnny Strachan's (Johnny Eh nae); he was my school chum and he died when he was about eight years old. I particularly remember that his whole school class attended the service and at the graveside we all sang 'There is a happy land'.

T.B. was a killer in those days and the treatment was pretty drastic, the patients being subjected to loads of fresh air, having to sleep with windows open or out on open-plan balconies, certainly a cure-or-kill remedy. Patients from St. Combs went as far south as Noranside in Angus.

There was also a very bad influenza epidemic during and just after the 1914 war, which claimed a few victims. My mother said that both my brother and I were very ill, my brother lying in one bed as if he was dead, whilst I was in another and quite delirious. Illnesses like measles, whooping cough, scarlet fever, mumps, spread through the village very rapidly. Diptheria claimed one of my contemporaries (Jimmy Robertson). The isolation hospital for St. Combs was at Strichen, where you had to spend six weeks in isolation, your parents looking through the windows when visiting.

By the turn of the century, cholera was eliminated and most of the other diseases are on the wane. Mothers and grannies could recognise the telltale signs of the illnesses even before the doctor came. Before the modern drugs came along, we sold many of the common medicines from the shop, i.e. castor oil, syrup of figs, cascara, ipecacuanha wine, Gregory's mixture, liquorice powder, olive oil, camphor oil, camphor blocks, eucalyptus oil, senna pod, lysol, aspirins, asthma cures, kidney and liver pills, stomach and headache powders, linseed oil, boracic lint, oiled silk, bandages, embrocations, etc., etc.

The fishermen suffered from salt-water boils and used to drink a mixture of salts and cream of tartar, and they also wore red woollen knitted wrist cuffs. They said this lessened the boils and had some preventative effect as well. During the winter there was a great demand for camphor blocks. These were slightly more than an inch square and about a quarter of an inch thick. The block was placed in a little bag and hung around the neck under the vest. This was supposed to act as a kind of disinfectant and prevent colds, flu, etc. Cod liver oil emulsion was also used to build up the children during the winter months. Chemical food was another tonic. Invalid diets would be gruel, fish soup, sweetbreads, beef tea, flour of meals and other patent concoctions. I remember this old first aider giving me instructions on how to restore a dislocated jaw. 'Pit yer twa thooms, intae the wicks of the bodies moo and birse until ye hear a snick.' A translation of this would be – 'Insert your two thumbs into each side of the patients's mouth and press until you hear a click.' I don't think I would have remembered it so well in this form.

This story was related to us by the doctor who was one of our instructors: this surgeon was walking down Union Street in Aberdeen when this chap was knocked down and his leg broken. The doctor went across to attend to the patient, but was pushed aside by a passing first aider. He strapped the lad up and, says the surgeon, made a far better job than he could have done in the circumstances.

The village weddings were a bit different from those of today. Some of the weddings were held in the Ban-Car Hotel at Lonmay, this being the nearest Hotel to the village, but most of the weddings would be held in the house. Some would be held in the church or local Kirky and the function held in the house. The mother of the house was more than likely to hold the purse strings and permission to wed would be addressed to her. Courting was a very secretive affair and only gradually filtered through to parents. The bridegroom would ask permission from the bride's parents and then approach his own for permission to wed. This incident relates to one such case:

Bridegroom – 'Midder, foo div I ston?'

Mither – 'Ston, sinny, ye ston on yer ain twa feet and if it wisna for my quintry creel, ye widna be stoning the wye ye ston.' It loses in translation but roughly it would be as follows: 'Mother, how do I stand financially?' Mother – 'You stand on your own two feet but if it wasn't for my efforts you wouldn't be as you are.' The more familiar one was – 'Can she bake, can she sew, can she make a moufu o' maet? If she can, then she'll dee.'

Everything having been settled and the wedding day fixed, there would be the calling of the bans, the beuking, claes carrying, feet washing, the blacking, the bedding, wedding procession, hansel. Wedding gifts would be shown in the best room in the house. The house or room to be occupied by the married couple would be prepared in the beuking and claes kerryin. The couple would have their feet washed and put in bed together, also any other couple who were known to be courting would get the same treatment. The bridegroom would have to face the blacking or tar and feather treatment.

The last Kirky wedding I remember was a cousin of my mother's. The groom came out of the house with his attendant and he threw a handful of coins to the waiting children, who scrambled to pick them up. It was also arranged that a woman would stand at the gate to collect a money gift from the groom (hansel). After the wedding ceremony has been performed by the minister in the Kirky, the company would walk back to the wedding house where the festivities would ensue. The meal would be similar to the walk meal: beef, broth, dumpling, steak pie, etc. There was one speciality which was called a bun (pastry) and berries. After the jollifications, fruit sweets would be handed out, the sweets would usually be dry sweets bought in half stone bags – pandrops, butternuts, Cupid whispers, conversation lozenges – and there would also be the continual serving of tea and fancy cakes (smachries).

Honeymoons were unknown and it was usually back to the daily drudge, cleaning the fireside, blackleading, washing, scrubbing, sheelin mussels, attending the boatie, baiting lines, etc. With the arrival of children women's chores increased, a cradle would often sit nearby the lines or nets to be rocked and send the bairn to sleep. When the bairn got older it might be put in a herring basket to frolic about. My granny with her huntle o' bairns seemed to thrive on it all and, even after her own brood left, took over the raising of two of her grandsons.

Dr. Trail was the regular Doctor for St. Combs before and after the 1914 war, and he used to come out to St. Combs on the train with his little black baggie. 'Sodom Helenie' was the midwife. Dr. Reid (Crimond) and Dr. McConnachie took over when Dr. Trail retired, but these have gone as well. Mrs. Bruce (Jean Jo) took over the midwife duties from Helenie but now district nurses are available. Also, there was no ambulance service but this has now been remedied as well. The elderly were mostly looked after by their families or were sent to Maud or Fraserburgh hospitals. Most of the refuse was dumped on the seashore on the braes or in the middens, any hard materials like limpets, mussels, cinders would be dumped in the street; but with the introduction of water, drains, lights and surfaced streets, the hygiene has improved and the endemic diseases are almost unknown so that the fiver (scarlet fever) – the mirrels (measles) – kink-hoast or croup (whooping cough) – T.B., etc., have become less of a problem. A refuse collection was also introduced so there was no need for middens or dumping rubbish in the street or on the seashore. The street lighting also helped to reduce accidents like tripping in the dark or bumping into each other. The children's pranks would also be reduced, as they would be more easily seen.

At the village weddings, the invitations were well spread. Minnie (Onack), already mentioned, got a lot of wedding invitations as she was apparently a generous present giver and, if she was unable to attend, she always sent a representative, as did Granny Mary. At this wedding her namesake and niece, Minnie West, was sent as her representative, whilst Granny Mary's representative was her son, John Clark. The celluloid collar (choker) was on the go at this time, it was about three inches deep and just about throttled you. Clark was being stubborn and was refusing to go as he was just about throttled like Hume, a prisoner who had recently been hung, but with his be-ribboned and be-laced sister, Minnie, they were both ushered to the feast. On entering the house they were greeted by an attendant: 'An fa are ye here for quinnie?' Minnie – 'I'm here for my Aunty Minnie.' 'An fa are ye here for, loonie?' 'I'm here for my midder Mary.' They were then ushered into the bun and berry feast.

At the claes kerry-ins there were usually some festivities and some who were not to be at the wedding attended it. This 'Claes Kerry-in' (clothes carrying) entailed carrying all the clothes and bits and pieces to the house the couple were to occupy, making the bed and putting all in order in the house.

The Nor-Easter

Cauld blaws the skirlin wild nor-easter
It scoors the roch and gurlie sea
It blaws fae Norway or Spitzbergen
And sooks the water fae the fame
Then spews it doon on the Buchan coast
It dampens claes and clorts the windaes
It stiffens up the shackle beens
And gies the auld angina jip

Nae south based finches lilten noo
They've fleed awa tae winter roosts
And left us wi' oor ain dull birdies
The craws, the gulls, the little spurgees.
The aulder folkies dreed the braes
And dinna venture far fae hame
They sit aleen at the ingle neuk
And lang for those warm simmer days.

And as each day oor time gets nearer
That wild nor-easter caulder gets
And ilka year a cronnie less
Nae mair to feel that cauld embrace.
There wis the time that we gid barfit
The thocht o' it noo makes me shiver
But seen I'll pit it a' tae richt
As I jist crawl atween the sheets
And switch that warmed up blanket aff.

Other Trades

I have mentioned most of the shops that were on the go during this period, but there were a few that started up and closed shortly afterwards. Some of the other trades in the village were builders, the Crannas, Patersons and Robertsons were masons, but none of their families followed in their footsteps. The joiners were William Bruce (Wull's son), who had his joiner's shop at the rear of his father's shop and he carried out work in Fraserburgh, Peterhead and Aberdeen and elsewhere. He also carried out undertaker's duties; he was followed in the trade by his sons and the business moved to Fraserburgh. William Cow (Buller) had his business in Charles Street but his business was on a smaller scale. My school chum, Sandy Buchan (Save), served his time with 'Buller'. The Buchan brothers (Zander and Zak) also carried out joinery work and operated from Fraserburgh. I remember Zak from the time he came to the house to get a hook taken out of his head. Some of the time-served joiners were Fleppy, Wulty, Wull's John, Save, Dave Cow, Johan's Sandy, Johan's John, Bulfer, who started in business in Peterhead in company with his son; other include Scott Cranna, Charlie West, Bruce (scoot Bob). The Forrests had a joinery business just a mile or so out of the village (The Vrichties).

The Fraserburgh toolworks employed many villagers and to name a few – Strachan (Katie's Jeck), Brucies John, Deef John, Peter Buzz, Fleppy's Sandy, Johnnie Lonnie, Peter Spotty, Poker, Mull, John Hay, etc. Some of these left for America, others to places in the south. There were plumbers, electricians, ship's carpenters, nurses, chemists, doctors, teachers, railway workers, domestic servants, quite a change from fishing and its associated trades. Some of the fishermen forsook the sea and started in other occupations.

J. Buchan (Diry Jim) went in for farming at Cairnglass Farm.

Bruce (Jonsie) took over the farm at Mosstown, Lonmay.

A. Buchan (Aithrie), Invernorth Farm, Rathen.

Bruce (Den o'Howie), the farm of Den o'Howie, Fetterangus.

Bruce (Buch) left the fishing and opened a shop near Keith.

P. Buchan (Plumber Patty) returned from America and started plumbing work when the water and drainage came to the village.

Charles West (Cha) was an engineer, then fisherman, then left the village and trained as an optician in London.

Several villagers were associated with fishing related jobs, as in kippering, canning, fish salesmen (Tans Charlie), Freshing (J. C. West), Fish Trade (Jack), Ship's Carpenter (Andra Perky) and Banker (John Hope).

One person who played a very important part in the village was Nan Buchan (Duncan's Nan). She was the music teacher (privately) and was organist or pianist at all the musical functions of the village. She was also a Sunday School teacher.

This is a short resumé of the changing character of the village, from being an almost totally-orientated fishing village to a mixed community. Similar transitions took place in Inverallochy and Cairnbulg. The golf course between the villages has been in use again and forms a common bond, as does the Free Mason Lodge – Inversaintcairn, the name embracing parts of the three villages. Most of the shops, mentioned already, have now closed or are under new ownership. The multi-stores in Fraserburgh and availability of cars to Aberdeen has reduced the local trade still further. The chip shop is still going strong. The village has lost a lot of its character and many of the old worthies have gone; the pace of today's world may be more efficient but the pleasure has gone. Often when I meet some of my old staff, it's the same old story – 'You wouldn't like it now, Davie, it's nae the same.' 'Roll on my pension' is their cry.

One family who left the village in my earlier life were the Buchan family from 10 High Street. The father was the village cobbler, a dummy and one of the 'Dood' family. His wife wasn't a local, they had two daughters who were also dummies, but didn't spend much time in the village. The Dummy had his workshop in an upstairs room and he had a sklate with a piece of skalie attached to it and you wrote your order on the slate, but he understood what you wanted just by pointing. His charges were sixpence for heels and one and sixpence for soles.

This anecdote was told to me by an engineer who was working on the land near the village. The land was to be taken over for use as a fighter airfield during the Second World War. George was doing some measure-

ments during one Sunday morning when this very irate local came up to
him and asked if he knew the fourth commandment. George knew pretty
well what he was getting at (Sabbath Day) but answered, 'Thou shalt not
commit adultery.' This further annoyed the mannie, who gave him a stern
lecture. George, not to be outdone, replied that he had no choice but to
work and if Hitler wasn't beaten none of us might be allowed to remember
the Sabbath day.

My father used to read the speaking parts in the 'cantates', etc., and
now this has been taking over by Alex Duncan (Buchan), a Sodomite.

The Ferm Servant

Noo Sandy wis a worken loon
He wis fee'd at Nether Loanie
He vrocht aa day and half the nicht
Tae take auld Loanie oot o' debt
Twas Sandy jist muck oot the byre
And Sandy jist ging strae the horse
And water her as weel.
Neist Sandy hid tae maet the hens
the dyeuks, the geese, the pigs
Then he took a load o' neeps
Tae scatter for the sheep.
Syne Loanie said jist take the horse
And ploo the widside perk.
Noo Meg the Horse wis auld and deen
Nae fit to ploo the widside perk
And Sandy he wis sae annoyed
He tackled Loanie aboot auld Meg
But didna come a bit o' speed
And said noo Loanie You'll have to get
Anither big strappen orra loon
I'll be leaving ye by the morn
Tae get anither kind o' job
For I couldna be coorse to my auld Meg.
Noo Sandy's chum fae Easter Loanie
Cried in on him neist day
And wi his shult and cairtie
Took Sandy to the nearby port
They went up and doon a ower the piers

Til they met up wi' Loanie's Jeemsie
Who took him on for jist a week
To see fou he could manage,
The week became a month and mair
And Sandy he wis hired
Tae fish wi' Loanie's Jeemsie's crew
A roon the herrin' fishin' ports.
Noo Jeems and Sandy they launched oot
An bocht anither muckle boat
Wi' oor Sandy at its helm.
The boat it did jist affa weel
Success it didna spoil him
But in a year or twa at most
He gid in for herren curen.
And noo wi money in his hands
He bocht oot auld Nether Loanie
Peer Meg the horse was deed and gone.
Tae places where deed horses go
Jist up the road a mile or twa
Tae auld Jock Sim, the knackers place.
Noo Sandy he wis gie weel kent
And wis voted tae the cooncil
And in anither year or twa
He wis made a cooncil baille
Oor Sandy wisna a bigsie chiel
He wis mindful of his roots
And of the years he did spend
As he tyauved at Nether Loanie
But fit came next jist foonert him
The cooncil made him Provost
Noo Sandy's in a fine big house
Wi twa big lamps set at his door
But aye he taks a turnie roon
Tae seem them a at Loanies.

Helpen Midder

A lot o little bairnies
Whose folkies were gie pushed
Hid tae help their mithers

Keep their heids abeen the sea:
Before the skweel, take oot the aise
Syne licht the biler fire
And fill the biler fou
Wi water fae the tank
Syne brush yer sheen
And kaim yer heid
And gie yer face a dicht.
His midder she wis watchen
Said, 'Nae cats lick here mi loon'
An took his head intae her hans
An scoored til his lugs were reed.
Syne up the road tae the skweel
As fast as his legs could tak him
His baggie on his little back
Gid dysten up and doon.
But on the wye he wis hinnert
His chums were playing bools
He rypet baith his pooches
Took out his twa-three bools
Then joined them in their gemmie
Til he lost a he hid
And hingin-lugget went tae skweel.
Ah weel, there's aye anither day
But kennen fine when the skweel cane oot
He'd start a ower again.
Its Billy chap some sticks and the scuttle fill wi coal
And Billy gin tae Aithries
For two pints o' mulk
Syne ging doon tae Patty's
For a Jamiesons new pan loaf
And Billy ging tae the wall
For a fracht o' clean fresh water
Or there will be nae supper ready
When yer fadder comes home fae sea.
Peer Billy he wis sae forfochen
He wisna fit to play
At fitba, bools or tackie
An didna jist feel richt
He took his supper wi the rest

But wis affa affa quaet
Crept up the stairs on his leen
An jist tumult inta bide.
His midder she came up the stairs
Tae see fit was wrang
He'd come oot in sic a rash
Peer Billy hid teen the mirrels.
Nae coal or sticks or water noo
He canna ging tae skweel
And Billy he jist laps it up
Wi gruel and juice and sweets
But best of all he did get
A bed a tae himsel.

A Buchan Loon

I was born on the 2nd January 1914 at 11 East Street, St. Combs, which was the largest shop in the village and was also the local Post Office. I went to the local village school when I was five and left the village school at eleven to go to the Fraserburgh Academy. I attended this academy for four years. When I was sixteen, I went to the Caledonian Wireless Collage in Edinburgh and left after gaining a Postmaster General Wireless Operator's Certificate. This was during the depression and there were no jobs available for operators. I returned to St. Combs with no job and wrote to several firms, including the R.A.F. I failed the R.A.F. test due to my eyesight. I then went into the shop and did odd jobs in the village and the hiring business.

In 1935 I was eventually successful in obtaining employment with the Post Office Engineering Department in Aberdeen on external construction work. After four months I was shifted to internal construction and after four months on this I was moved to Peterhead as a maintenance engineer. I was given a small green van and with no experience told to get on with it.

At the telephone exchange at this time there were three females during the day and a male for night duties. The supervisor was Megg Hutton assisted by Amy Mackie and another young lady, Margaret Duthie (Rita), who was to become my wife some time later.

I was pretty green at the job, not yet having been a year at this work, but I managed to get by. Under a reorganisation programme, I was shifted to Huntly in 1937. I enjoyed my spell there but, in October 1938, my father and niece were killed and my sister-in-law seriously injured. On compassionate grounds, I was moved back to Peterhead and was able to travel home at night to help my mother sort things out in the shop.

In 1939, I went to London on a defence course, as the signs of war were evident. In August 1939 I was stationed in a Defence Station in Orkney, which was the central point for all defence establishments in the Orkneys, including Scapa Flow. I was on duty the night the *Royal Oak* was torpedoed in Scapa. In 1940 I was back in Aberdeen working in what was called the Repeater Station. I had several courses on various aspects pertaining to the job. I was also used on Army Liaison Duties and R.A.F. tuition duties (1940–1945).

In 1946 the Peterhead-Norweign submarine was to be re-opened and it required someone with Morse qualifications, which I had, so I was once again back to Peterhead, taking my wife back to her home town. I spent several nights in the Gaddle Braes cable hut. I stayed there until 1954, when I returned to Aberdeen as an Assistant Executive Engineer on external planning and travelled widely over the Aberdeen area.

I was promoted to Executive Engineer and moved to Dundee, staying in Carnoustie. My wife took ill at this time and the doctors advised to try and get back to Aberdeen. I was successful in getting a transfer. My wife's health improved slightly but in 1976, due to my wife's health, I retired after forty years' service, which on the whole, I enjoyed, in spite of the shifts and ups and downs.

I always kept in touch with St. Combs, especially when my mother was in the shop, and after she retired to live in what was known as the butcher's half house. I was asked several times to go south to various posts, but due to domestic circumstances, was unable to accept. Most of my cronnies have now departed the scene and there isn't the same incentive to visit the auld toonie.

With this brief resumé of an ordinary Buchan Loon's life, I will close this rather personalised Buchan story.

Bye The Day

And now my Buchan tale has ended
To auld lang syne I look eence mair
And wish I were that young again
Wi' barfit feet, tae tred those beaches
Wi' toosled hair and patched up breeches
A jeely piece, or tattie scone
I hinna time for that or yon
The tides near oot, my linies dry
I rin like mad to save my fry

Those squawking gulls will hae my trooties
I'm just in time to save the flukies
The diving brutes, they hae nae manners
But they're too late, they're for the branner.

It's bye the day, nae linies noo
The yawlies idle, their days are ower
They're broken up to stoke the fire
And faurs the creels, the piecie boxies
The waitin' wifies, wyvin socks
Nae mair, nae mair, its bye the day
A box o' cod fae Rattray Bay
Bob Boothy's ashes scattered wide
Faur are they noo, it's bye the day
The trainies gone, the station too
It's thanks to him – to you know who
The village it's changed, the folkies too
It's bye the day, it's bye the day.

Wullie's Dog

Fin I got up this mornen
And opened oor ootside door
Tae see fit like the widder wis
And if we could gyan tae sea
There wis oor cattie lying there
Aa stiff and caal and deed
Fa wid dee sic an affa thing
It maun hae been that dog o' Wullie's.

The butcher's maun be killen
For there's an affa dogs aboot
Aye on the look oot for scraps
Tae full their teem stamicks
Bit fa hid left the coos fit
Richt on oor door step
It maun hae been that dog again
Aye oor Wullie's dog nae doot.

Oor bickie is nivver aff the chine
At that certain time
Unless she's oot wi me
She's nivver awa fae hame
But fa did faither her fulpies
That came upon the scene
Aye it maun be him again
That affa dog o' Wullie's.

Abody kent oor Wullie's dog
For he wis aye there or thereaboots
Gweed kens jist fan the cratur sleepit
For he wis aye on the scran
A bit o' cheese, a jeely piece
It aa gid doon like lichtnin
It wisna easy come and it wisna easy going
His life hid aye been, jist ae lang trauchle.

But Wullie's dog it wis missen
For twa or three days at least
And Wullie's neepers gid in bye
And there wis Wullie on the fleer
He'd been deed for a day or mair
Oor Wullie's dog wis at his heid
Gein Wullie's caal face an antrin lick .
Bit the peer doggie got, no response at aa.

A neeper took the doggie hame
And named the dog Wullie
The doggie nivver had a name
For he wis just Wullie's doggie
The wifie was awfa gweed tae Wullie
Bit the doggie he gid aff his maet
And the peer cratur jist dwined awa
He coudna live, withoot his maister Wullie.

Anither Spik

Shaemus and his wife Kathleen
They settled in the Broch

They hid come fae the Emerald Isle
Fae a toonie near Belfast
Noo Hamish as his freens aye caaed him
He liked 'The Crater' gweed and strong
But sometimes he gid ower the tap
And feenished in a gie bit tizzie
This nicht in his favourite haunt
He sang some Irish rebel sangs
And some folk there jist didna like it
The result there wis a gie bit stushie
And oor peer Hamish wis helpit oot
Then neist day twa Broch bobbies
They chappit on oor Kathleen's door
She asked the bobbies tae come in
And poored a drap o' her poteen
They asked her if her man wis in
And Kathleen said na, that he wis oot
Then they asked what wis his wark
He's warked for 'Jaezus' for some time
He maun be a preacher chiel
A minister or priest perhaps
No, no, he's no, he works for Jeyes fluid.
Wi' that the bobbies got up tae go
Jist tell yer man tae look in bye.
Oor Hamish he just got a warning
And disna blot his copy book noo.

A Penny in the Slot

There wis a bad depression
In the nineteen twenty/thirties
And mony folkies fae the toonies
Packet their baggies and left their hames
To look for work in foreign pairts.
There wis this canny chielly
Watchen a' the folkies leaven
But couldna mak his mind up fit tae dee
When his best pal departed
He decided to gie it a go
And wi his baggie on his back

He set aff for the mighty States.
He boarded a boatie in the Clyde
But the crossen it was affa coorse
And he hardly left his bunk at aa
When he landed in America
He wis still gyan up and doon
And his stamick and his heid were affa bad
Wi a penny in his han he made for a toilet
But his penny widna ging in the slot
He tellt a mannie in a shoppie fit wis wrang
The mannie said his money was nae ees
In the great and mightly States
It wis dollars, cents and dimes
That were need in that land.
But oor peer New Town chielly
And the wye that he wis feelen
He'd hid eneuch of the mighty U.S.A.
The mannie in the shoppie
Said, 'Seeing you are a Scot
You can use my toilet free of charge.'
And when he was a bittie better
He made straight for a boatie hame
And got anither roch crossen comen back
But this time when he landed
His penny gid in the slot
A blessen tae ben back in Bonnie Scotland.
When he got back tae the Broch,
He got a jobbie wi a curer
Makken kits and barrels and boxes
For the comen herren season.
He nivver ventures far, or envies them that leave
For he aye mines on the affa affa crossens
And the time his penny widna fit the slot.
They can hae the might States
Their dollars and their dimes
I'll just bide at hame
Where a penny gings in the slot.

The Cairty

When I wis young and hairty
I hid a horse and cairty
The cairty broke, a wheel came off
And I fell oot the cairty
Wi a lot o' cuts and sairties.

They took me hame and patched me up
Wi cloots and bits o' plaister
And I wis sair for days on end
I lost some teeth, my moo wis swalt
My een were black and blue

The horsie got an affa fleg
And ran till he wis stoppit
The peer wee beastie hirpled hame
And wise happit wi his plaidie
Wit the doggies nestled there beside him.

The vet he came tae see the pony,
But the doggies didna like him
They widna let the mannie in
And he hid jist, tae come, tae me
Tae takk him tae the pony.

The mannie said he'd hurt his fit
But in a day or twa he'd be
As richt as rain tae yoke again
The doggies wid be affa shuited
Tae rin wi their freen the pony.

The Invitation

Come on noo a ye Buchan folk
I'm sure ye can a better me
And write aboot yer ain folk
That ye a kent sae lang ago
There's stories that I've forgotten
And ithers that jist waurna richt

Come on noo, Sandy, Jeck and Alick,
Think up yer thumpers and dinna be blate
There's a hantle beuks that hiv been written
Aboot a the places roon bonny Deeside
Nae doot that wifie in Balmoral
Maun hae a lot tae dee wi that.
We hinna hulls like the Grampian mountains
Or rivers like the Dee and Don
But fit aboot oor ain wee hullies
The Tillyduff and Mormond Braes
These twa hullies are affa handy
Fin shotten lines, yer troonks or nets
For getten tae the hanlin spotties
Aff Rottra Heid on the Buchan coast.
Come on noo, Sandy, Alick and Jeck,
Tak up yer pens and paper quick
And tak a trip doon memory lane
Tak aff yer sheen and wheelen drawers
And rin aboot – feel yung again
Forget about sair shackle beens.
Angina, hoasts, yer water works,
I'm sure it will fess tae yer hairt
Fin ye jist start tae pit it doon
Come on noo, Sandy, Alick and Jeck,
Take up yer pens and paper quick
And pit it doon in black and fite
Afore this earth ye quit for gweed.

The Pension

A lot o New Toon folkies
Were Liberals oot and oot
Some whose convictions were so strong
They named their bairns efter him
The him that led the Liberals aa his life
That grite little mannie fae Wales
Sir David Lloyd George the wizard
He hid a lot tae dee wi the pension
Maybe that's fou they were sae Liberal
Gweed Kens fou the folkies managed

In the days before the pension came
But in the early pension days
That wis every Friday mornen sharp
Some aal folkies wid be waiten there
For the Post Office shoppie door tae open
To get their pension ten shillen note
And tae get there twa or three eerins
In case the money wid rin oot.
It took a whiley for it to register
That the pension money widna ging deen
And that life wid be that bittie better.
The pension noo bears nae relation
To the time o that aal ten shillen note
The Welsh mannies awa nae yet forgotten
But the Friday mornen folkies
That stood at the shoppie door
Are gone and lang forgotten.

Glossary

a	– all	bark	– tanning for nets
aa	– all	been	– bone
aal	– old	beetle durks	– robust boots
abeen	– above	beets	– boots
abody	– everybody	beuk, buick,	
aboot	– about	byeuk	– books
ae	– one	bichie	– female dog
ahin	– behind	biggit	– built
ahint	– behind	biles	– boils
ails	– troubles	bocht	– bought
ain	– own	bools	– marbles or bowls
aise	– ashes	boot twa faal	– bent double
ambree	– cupboard	boozer	– late train
Andra	– Andrew	breeks, bricks	– trousers
anint	– beside	Brick Wall	– local well
anither	– another	braws	– best clothes
aroon	– around	bum	– rear end
awfa, affa	– awful	but and bens	– rooms in house
auld	– old	busket	– dressed
aye	– yes	B.W.T.A	– British Women's
			Temperance
ba	– ball		
bade	– told	caen	– calling
baggies	– bags for clothes	cairt	– cart
baldies	– small boats	caff	– chaff
bandies	– sticklebacks	caffsecks	– bolsters
barfit	– bare-footed	Cample,	–

147

Campill,	–		donner	–	small marbles
Camphill	–	shore	dook	–	bathe
canny	–	careful	doon	–	down
canna	–	cannot	doorstep	–	thick slice
canon	–	large marble	douce	–	slice
chap	–	mash, chap, hit	drawers	–	underpants
chappers	–	mouth	draygen	–	kite
chappit	–	knocked, mashed	droon	–	drown
chiel, chielly	–	person or fellow	durks	–	shoeware
chines	–	chains	dumfounert	–	amazed
chucken	–	chicken	dyen	–	doing
claes	–	clothes			
claes poles	–	drying poles	earins, eerins	–	errands
claik	–	news	een	–	eyes
claith	–	cloth	eence	–	once
clocken	–	broody	ena	–	as well
cloot	–	cloth	eneuch	–	enough
clorts	–	covers			
coo	–	cow	fa	–	who
cotten wadden	–	cotton wool	fadder, faither	–	father
cowbel	–	cobble	fae	–	from
cowpin ladle	–	see-saw	far and faur	–	where
cowpit	–	upset	fardens,		
coothie	–	warm, homely	farthing	–	biscuit
current	–	currant	farens	–	ginger slice
cut	–	wool	fashed	–	troubled
		measurement	fau	–	who
			fecht	–	fight
darkie	–	kite	fessen up	–	brought up
danders	–	cinders	filey	–	while
deed	–	dead	fin	–	when
deen-up	–	done up	fit	–	foot
delse	–	edible seaweed	fitba	–	football
dicht	–	clean, wipe	fite	–	white
dichtet	–	sprinkled	flee cemetery	–	currant slice
dinna	–	don't	fleed	–	flown
diry	–	dairy	fleer	–	floor
dirler	–	toy (rasping	fleg	–	frighten
		noise)	flukies	–	flounders
Dody	–	George	folkies	–	people

fooed	–	filled	hanlin	– hand line
forbye	–	as well	hansel	– gift
fordel	–	store	happet	– covered
fou	–	how	hantle	– a lot
fower	–	four	hawlen	– hauling
fracht	–	two pails	heed on win	– head wind
full butt	–	full speed	helster gowdie	– head over heels
fulpies	–	pups	hert, hairt	– heart
fummer	–	toy	his	– has
furler	–	toy propeller	hiv	– have
fussle	–	whistle	hoosies	– houses
			howket	– dug
gallus	–	gallows braes	hummer	– toy
gelly	–	galley	huns	– hounds
geen	–	given	himist	– last
geen tae, gite	–	gone to pot	hooses	– houses
gid	–	went		
gi, gie	–	give	ill tricket	– mischievous
ging	–	go	ingen	– onion
girdle	–	griddle	ingle neuk	– fireside
girnen	–	whimpering	inta	– into
gin tae gite	–	go to pot	in timmers	– internal organs
glaiket	–	simple	is	– this
Glesga	–	Glasgow	instide	– instead
gless	–	glass	ither	– other
glesser	–	glass marble		
gotten	–	got	Jannie	– Janitor
gowden	–	golden	jeelies	– jellies
gowket	–	silly	jist	– just
gurly	–	tempestuous	joogfu	– jugful
gyan	–	going		
gyen	–	gone	kaim	– comb
			kirky	– church
hae	–	have	kerry	– carry
haet	–	hot	kerry-in	– carrying
had	–	hold	ken	– know
hame	–	home	kennen	– knowing
hameower	–	homely	kent	– knew
han	–	hand	kicket	– kicked
hanfae	–	handful	kicks	– weeds

Kirsten	– Christian	mishanters	– mistakes
kink-hoast	– whooping cough	mitten	– glove
kist	– trunk	mixter maxter	– mixed lot
kittlins	– kittens	mou	– mouth
kniffie	– knife game	moufa	– mouthful
		mowse	– not safe
labster	– lobster	muckle	– large
lach	– laugh	muck mudden	– currant slice
lidder	– along		
laeder	– hurry	na, naw	– no
lang	– long	nae	– not
leader	– main herring	neebor,	
	rope	neeper	– neighbour
lean, leen	– alone	newsd	– talked
Leeby	– Elizabeth	nicht	– night
lickens	– thrashings	nive	– fist
lilten	– singing		
linies	– seashore lines	oo	– wool
linners	– vests	oor	– our
loons	– boys	oot	– out
loup	– jump	on't	– on it
louper dogs	– porpoise	oorsels	– ourselves
lowse	– loose	ony	– any
		ordner	– ordinary
maesel	– myself	our, ower	– too
maest	– most		
maet	– meat	pairt	– part
makk	– make	pairted,	
mair	– more	pairten	– apportioned
man or maun	– must	partens	– edible crab
mannie	– man	peels	– crabs for bait
Masons Meer	– trestles	peels	– pills
meenits	– minutes	peeries	– taps
meggens	– mercy	Peet	– Peter
menners	– manners	peety	– pity
midden	– rubbish tip	pent, pint	– paint
Midder,		perk	– park
mither	– mother	pillers	– crab bait
mine	– remember	pookly,	
mirrels	– measles	puckly	– small amount

pooches	–	pockets	selt	–	sold
poodery	–	powdery	siccar	–	hold strongly
pooren	–	pouring	shackle beens	–	joints
press	–	cupboard	Shanks's pony	–	walking
			sheen	–	shoes
queeties	–	sea birds	sheelen	–	emptying
queets	–	ankles	shewder,		
quine	–	girl	shouder	–	shoulder
quintry	–	country	shores	–	beach landings
quities	–	dresses	shuited	–	suited
			siller	–	money
ravelt	–	topsy-turvey	siree, soirée	–	concert
revelt	–	untidy	skalie	–	slate pencil
reed	–	red	skelp	–	slap
red chicket	–	red-cheeked	sklate	–	slate
reef	–	roof	skirlen	–	screaming
redden	–	untangling	skull	–	line basket
redd steens	–	anchoring stones	sma	–	small
richt	–	right	smaalin	–	small line
riggen oot	–	getting ready	smachries	–	fancy cakes
riggen tile	–	roof	smiddy	–	blacksmith shop
rin	–	run	snick	–	click
ringle-e	–	wall eyed	snoot	–	peak
rippers	–	fishing line	soddy	–	game
roch	–	rough	sods	–	turf
Rottra	–	Rattray	sooks	–	sucks
rug	–	pull	soor	–	sour
			sooth	–	south
sae	–	so	spads	–	spades
saftie	–	soft biscuit	span	–	handmeasure
sair	–	much	speens	–	spoons
sair	–	sore	spellen	–	spelling
sannel	–	sand eels	spews	–	vomits
sanny	–	sandy	spurgies	–	sparrows
sappus	–	crab lure	spy-glass	–	binocular
sark	–	shirt			telescope
saut	–	salt	stamick	–	stomach
scran, scrann	–	scrounge	stank	–	ditch
seen	–	soon	steelers	–	steel marbles
segs	–	broad grass	steys	–	corsets

Steenhive	– Stonehaven	Umman	– woman
steens	– stones	uphull	– cake like a hill
stocken laff	– laughing stock		
stockens	– stockings	vrang	– wrong
stoker	– cash	vratch	– wrongdoers
ston, stan	– stand	vrocht	– worked
strae, stray	– straw	vrechties	– joiners
straint	– strained		
strappen	– well-built	wadden	– wedding
streen	– yesterday	wardle	– world
stripe	– stream	Wast	– West
strippen	– stripping	waurna	– weren't
sweem	– swim	wee	– little
swye, swey	– swivel	weel	– well
		weirt	– wear
tackets	– studs	Wellum, Wull,	
tae	– to	Wulzie	– William
tee	– also	welks, wulks	– winkles
tanner	– sixpence	whars	– where is
tappit	– tapped	whellan	– wool
teem	– empty	whit	– what
thocht	– thought	wi	– with
titler	– toy	widder	– weather
Tillyduff	– hill	widna	– wouldn't
tippens	– twisted hair	wisna	– wasn't
toppers	– knee boots	worsit	– knitting wool
toon	– town	wye	– way
toorie	– tassle	wyvin, wiven	– knitting
toppers	– knee boots		
tottery	– unsteady	yalla	– yellow
tousled	– unruly	yawl, yowl	– boat
tows	– ropes	ye	– you
trunks,		yer	– your
troonks	– crab traps	yersel	– yourself
trappit	– trapped	Yirned milk	– curds and whey
trauchle	– struggle	yoke	– for carrying
truncher	– platter		water – harness
trauchle	– struggle		
twa	– two	yon	– those
twal	– twelve	youkie,	
thumpers	– brains	yowkie	– itchy